IPSWICH ZERO 6

Ray Hollingsworth

Personal and alternative experiences before,

during and after The S

SKY NEWS

Published by Sparkfilms

5 Durham Square, Colchester, Essex, CO1 2RS

United Kingdom.

First published in Great Britain

as a paperback original in 2011 by Sparkfilms

A CIP catalogue record for this book is available
from the British Library.

ISBN 978-0953695843

IPSWICH ZERO 6

This is a collection of different forms of writing that were produced before, during and after the serial killings of five young women in Ipswich.

This project was the result of revisiting my research into the scene at Ipswich after I was contacted by a gentleman who had some very different ideas to the police and authorities on the case.

It took me back into the pages of text, scripts, interviews and poetics that I had left as work in progress - which at that stage may never have been released in any form.

My intention was to produce something between a book, a media pack and a kind of document. It turned out as more of a book.

I often have music on in the background while I am working. Bands that carried me through the last few years include Razorlight, White Lies, Hard Fi and The Enemy.

Sometimes I would drive back from Ipswich in the early hours with 'Somewhere Else' by Razorlight on repeat play.

SKY NEWS

Mediascape

The media journal that relates to December 2006 was written in February 2010. It is written in short paragraphs, the intention being, to take the reader through it quickly.

The subheadings were an afterthought. I considered the writing was perhaps too 'off the cuff' as it were, and that the subheads would add a little texture and guidance, that is, if anyone should ever read it.

Voices

Some of the interviews with 'working girls' took place between the summer of 2005 and spring of 2006. It was also an after-thought to add subheads to this section - very unusual for an interview styled piece.

Sometimes an answer from a girl of just a few words could evoke a hint of an entire life story, that is how I saw it anyway. It occurred to me that a random list of some of these statements might give a viewer or reader the desire to look a little deeper. I found myself looking deeper into their lives.

SPARKFILMS

Soundscape

I wrote the 'soundscape' between walking the dog and shampooing carpets in March 2010. It's a made up from a selection of linked poetic pieces and ideas. As it stands it is a kind of work in progress that may never go further than these pages.

Poetics

The poetry stuff was written between the summer of 2005 and some-time in 2007. My aim is to write as quickly as possible, putting down what were mostly personal experiences and trying in my own way to convey the moments as they happened - reproduced as glimpses, snapshots.

SPARKFILMS

Filmscape

The base / draft filmscript was put together in the months
before the first of the girls went missing. I saw incredible
life stories being 'acted out' on these streets. This was the
underbelly of British subculture being played out for a select
audience who could never have imagined what was about to unfold.

Reflections

The Reflections section was originally called 'Extras' and only
consisted of a few pieces about television programmes based on
the murders. I decided to take a look a some of the scientific
issues in the case that were discussed at the trial, and
inaddition to this, a number of other aspects surrounding the
scene in Ipswich. While I was writing this section I learned of
the tragic and lonely death of Philippa Walker.

SPARKFILMS

Mediascape

Missing Girl In Ipswich

My friend Susan said one evening 'have you heard about the missing girl in Ipswich?'. I said I hadn't.

Susan would not have known that I had been researching the twilight underworld of Ipswich for a draft filmscript before we met.

Additionally, I had written a kind of poetic journal mirroring the backdrop to the scene there.

The beginnings of this work were released in a poetry book called 'Dirty Blonde at the Cash Machine' in March 2006.

Because of the nature of my work I decided to send a copy of the book and the framework of the filmscript to the press office at Suffolk Police.

I was describing the backdrop to an extraordinary seedy underworld in what was perceived to be a fairly ordinary market town in East Anglia.

It would surprise me if the police had taken much notice of what I had sent them, although I doubt they would have seen anything like it before.

Surreal Netherland

It occurred to me that there was some kind of story to tell and I wanted to create something that was somehow poetically ambient and atmospheric that could transport people into this surreal netherland.

The writing that I had been compiling would not have been possible without spending time with some of the girls who were fueling their drug habits by working on the streets of Ipswich.

Gradually I was able to build a profile of their lives. It was possible to build a timeline of their daily lives from conversations in my car or at my Colchester home.

I used to tell them I was writing about their lives. None of them complained, and if anything, I think they found it interesting.

At some stage I had contacted the vice squad in Ipswich as I thought they should know of my work. They had offered to give me a guided tour of the area which would have included the massage parlours.

We never got around to the tour but I appreciated that they must have considered the scene worthy of some kind of written observation.

I got the impression that there was a certain kind of understanding and perhaps an element of tolerance between some of the police and the working girls.

This is not to say that the police were not monitoring the area. They were. But they did so in a way that was both legal and fair.

There is no doubt that in many cases the girls were dealt with through the courts for their activities on the streets or through shop lifting.

Anneli Alderton

I know this because Anneli Alderton had spoken openly about her life and described her court appearances and time in prison.

Ms Alderton was incredibly open and honest about her life and something occurred during the time that I spent with her that was to haunt me some months later.

I hadn't really taken much notice of the missing girl in Ipswich at this stage. I saw her picture on the local news but Tania Nicol was unknown to me.

At that stage I think she had been missing for a few weeks but this didn't really amount to much. My assumption was that she might be in a different part of the country.

It was obvious that any girl who plies her trade on dimly lit streets would be vulnerable to some form of abduction, yet this seemed to be a rare occurrence.

From a personal point of view there was an overlap to an abduction theory as I had been adding a new dimension to my filmscript that involved girls being taken off the Ipswich streets by a European gang and bundled into the back of white vans.

This element to the film draft was not included in my work in progress that I had sent to Suffolk Police. The idea had come from references to a group of Kosovan exiles who were known to treat the girls badly.

I had taken parts of this knowledge and added my own fictional story line that introduced a Kosovan base at a farm and outbuildings that they had taken control of somewhere in the Suffolk outback.

The story line was in no way 'off radar' in the circumstances and, for all I know, may have been one of the possibilities the police were later to consider during their enquiries.

The Merging of Fantasy and Reality

It was always possible to come up with ideas for the film by joining up the dots from conversations with the girls. My ideas were based on part reality and part fantasy, but the fictional aspect always seemed close to unravelling and nothing I had written seemed too far fetched.

Then something happened that alerted me to the possibility that the events aligned to my story might just be happening for real. Another girl was reported missing. Once again, I had no knowledge of a girl by the name of Gemma Adams.

I started to follow the local news much more closely. There was the sense that there could be some kind of connection to the disappearance of two girls from what would seem to be common territory.

As I hadn't been to Ipswich for a few months I was a little off pace with the scene whose players were a transient group of women and drug dealers who lived their lives in a completely different way to anything known to most of the public.

It was this different way of life with its instincts of survival and feeding a habit that had interested me so much, and it would be quite fair to say that I was building some kind of obsession with this form of alternative living.

I felt compelled to write about it, and although the closer scrutiny had occurred some months before the disappearances, I considered that my knowledge of the area and how it worked might be of some help to the police.

Discovery of a Body

The next development was to be the dramatic news of the tragic discovery of the body of Gemma Adams. This sent an immediate message to me that said 'serial killer'.

Initial police reports were careful not to link the find of Ms Adams with the disappearance of Tania Nicol but I don't doubt they feared the worse.

Then came the announcement that confirmed another body to be that of Tania Nicol. Several days later a third body was discovered and I think it was at this stage that the huge media interest suddenly escalated to a national and global level.

From this moment my life was going to change but it was still several days before I would become involved with the media in what would become one of the most reported news stories in British media history.

I became particularly concerned for 'Katie' who I had lost touch with and suddenly decided to drive down to Ipswich to see if I could find her. By doing so, I realised that I was exposing myself to CCTV and police scrutiny but that did not deter me.

Killing Grounds at Midnight

The one thing that concerned me was the safety of those girls. I don't think I was alone in feeling that way. To drive into an area after midnight where a serial killer might be operating was a chilling and eerie experience.

At around 1am I saw a girl standing in West End Road who I later believed from descriptions to be Paula Clennell. I never knew for sure if it was her but I gave this information to the police in the following days.

I became pre-occupied with the events in Ipswich. They were taking over my life at a time when I had just committed to some casual employment.

As a small time writer I was living hand to mouth and had to do a number of casual jobs to make ends meet. I was two days into the most excruciating and mind numbing experience I had ever endured during my working life.

I found myself on a 6am till 2pm shift in a book distribution depot about a 25 minute drive away. It didn't take me too long to realise that I had entered into some kind of mind torture chamber.

That morning, just after I arrived, I saw a group of people leaving who had just finished the night shift. It is a scene I will not forget. They looked like zombies. Staring out ahead with glazed eyes and fixed expressions.

My impression was that they were mainly Eastern Europeans. I remember thinking...if I look like this after 8 hours in this place it will kill me.

I didn't make the 8 hour shift. At around 11.30 the news came on the radio above that another woman had been reported missing in Ipswich. I thought, right, that's it, I need to do something.

Getting Away from the Zombies

I went up to the supervisor and just said something like - 'I'm sorry, I just need to get out of here', he seemed surprised but allowed me to leave which I did as quickly as possible, and I would never return. On the drive back home my mind was racing, I felt I had a connection to what was happening in Ipswich. The

SKY NEWS

events had suddenly engulfed me and with my background knowledge I decided I should contact the media myself.

When I got home I switched on the TV. The latest developments from Ipswich were on Sky News and I decided to fire off an email to them offering an insight into the backdrop to the scene in Ipswich.

I mentioned my writing and research and to my amazement they replied in a matter of minutes and asked if I would be prepared to appear on The Martin Stanford programme that evening.

This all happened at around 3 in the afternoon on December 12th. Sky offered to pick me up in a car in Colchester and speed me off to the Sky News Centre in Isleworth which must have been about 75 miles away.

I spoke to a producer on the telephone and said I was quite prepared to make my own way there by train and taxi link. This was agreed and I was just asked to report to reception when I arrived with a view to getting there around 7ish.

After getting changed I set off from Colchester and after a three hour journey I found myself in view of all the Sky buildings in Grant Way, Isleworth.

To this day I do not possess a mobile telephone and during my journey I would not have been aware of any developments in this fast moving story.

Walking into Sky News Reception

When I walked into Sky News reception I was in shock as I looked up at the screens. Another two bodies had been discovered in Ipswich that afternoon while I was travelling up from Colchester.

A producer came down to meet me and I remember saying to him that due to this desperately sad news I could quite understand if my input would be overshadowed and I was prepared to make my way back home.

He told me my input would be even more valuable as they had planned me in to a revised schedule that would concentrate entirely on the news from Ipswich.

Things had developed so quickly that Sky must have dropped The Martin Stanford show that evening to cover what was becoming one of the biggest crime stories in British media history.

I was ushered into a 'make-up' room along with several others. At this stage I had little idea what was coming next although I had worked out that I was shortly to speak live in front of an audience of millions.

Things had moved so quickly that there was no time to feel nervous.

Suddenly I found myself sitting in front of the cameras in a setting that had grown familiar to me on my television screen.

I recognised newscaster Steve Dixon but I did not realise who the lady was who was sitting next to me. We sat there for a couple of minutes while an ad break ran through, then it started.

Next I could see Jeremy Thompson on a screen speaking from Suffolk Constabulary at Martlesham Heath. Mr Thompson somehow made it very comfortable to converse and exchange dialogue.

Talking about the girls to an Audience of Millions

I was able to speak about the girls in a way that looked deeper into their lives and their journeys into a drug fueled existence. It was an opportunity to mention the interviews I had conducted with some of them and how I felt an empathy towards them.

One of the aspects of their lives that I touched on was that they had all been toddlers at one stage and how life's journey can go so wildly off course.

After speaking for a few minutes Jeremy Thompson directed a question to the lady sitting next to me and it was not until that moment that I realised who she was.

My Respect for Rosie Boycott

Rosie Boycott was known to me through Newsnight Review and I was aware that she had been the editor at both The Independent and Sunday Independent.

During the time we were speaking there were chilling tag lines running across the bottom of the screen 'TWO BODIES FOUND NEAR LEVINGTON, SOUTH OF IPSWICH' and 'SUFFOLK KILLER: POLICE INVESTIGATING THREE MURDERS FIND TWO MORE BODIES'.

Stark images of the streets in the red light area and the scene at Levington continued as a haunting backdrop throughout the broadcast.

During an advertising break I noticed how the newscaster was texting his wife from his mobile phone.

The exchanges continued and I was able to express my amazement that the last two girls appeared to have been taken off the streets right under the police gaze.

Rosie Boycott shared my view. She said that she didn't believe the girls had been properly protected by the police.

The conversations continued for some time and we touched on possible profiles of a serial killer and references to The Yorkshire Ripper.

Ms Boycott mentioned that historically most men who were apprehended for violent incidents against prostitutes had a previous track record.

The interviews came to a close and I felt we were allowed to speak openly and expressively and were able to give the viewers something worthwhile.

We went to what is known as a Green Room and had a kind of de-brief. The producer said the telecast had gone out to a huge audience and that Sky were very pleased with how it went.

I asked Rosie Boycott for her address which she was happy to give. I later sent her a book with an inscription that expressed the great respect I had for her.

Sky asked me if I would be prepared to do other pieces in the next few days to which I agreed.

They arranged for a car to take me back to Liverpool Street.

I arrived home about midnight and switched on to Sky News. The story was dominating everything. At around 2am I finally went to bed wondering if I would get to sleep as my mind was racing with sounds and images from the last 12 hours.

The following morning I was up at 7am. The news was streaming through all the news channels.

The telephone started around 8.30 and went pretty much non stop through the day. Everyone was switched on to this story.

Media Frenzy

It must be quite easy for media types to contact you when your name is on a television screen and you say you live in Colchester. Maybe they use 'Directory Enquiries'.

Anyway, whatever way they track you down I suddenly had a diary that was pretty much full for the next 48 hours.

It didn't occur to me at the time that I may have been able to negotiate some payment for some of the contacts I was able to put national newspapers in touch with.

Things were moving at break neck speed. The day passed in a blur. At around 8pm things had calmed down a little and I decided to drive down to Ipswich and see if I could meet up with Jeremy Thompson in person.

It was apparent by now that there was a huge media presence encamped at Suffolk Police HQ in Martlesham and I thought it might offer an opportunity to meet up with some of the people who had contacted me.

So off I went down the A12. Martlesham is about a 40 minute drive away and before I knew it I had driven into the complex and parked up.

It never occurred to me when I drove through the unmanned gates that I didn't have anything like a police pass or a press pass. It was a subject that would come up later though.

There were television and radio vehicles everywhere you looked. Each of them seemed to be situated in a neat space that afforded room to walk around. News stories were going out live as I carefully stepped over cables and looked for the Sky van.

Drinking Coffee from Plastic Cups

After a few minutes I found it along with a huddle of guys who were drinking coffee from plastic cups. I introduced myself to Jeremy Thompson and he seemed surprised to but pleased to see me.

I also met Sky crime correspondent Martin Brunt and the three of us discussed future Sky coverage and how I could give them further insight into the area.

After speaking for a short while we noticed a large convoy of police cars slowly moving towards the exit gate about 75 yards away. It was an unusual and eerie sight.

For a moment none of us seemed to realise what we were witnessing or the significance of it. I think it was Martin who worked out that these were the police cars with specialist number plate recognition capabilities that were about to be deployed in the red light area and surrounds.

I think these cars had been commissioned from Merseyside Police, but to my mind, they had arrived far too late.

It was very interesting having the opportunity to speak to Jeremy and Martin off-screen and I think we all realised that we were involved in different ways of reporting something of epic proportions in British crime history.

After about 40 minutes it was time to leave the media compound. Martin Brunt and I exchanged phone numbers and email details which were to prove very useful in the days ahead.

I drove back to Ipswich which was about 5 miles from the police HQ and parked at Sainsbury's which is close to the area where the girls were working.

It was a few minutes walk away from the red light area and I wanted to take a look around and see what the streets were like with a serial killer at large and what the police presence was like at close quarters.

SKY NEWS

I stopped by at a parked squad car and briefly explained my interest and to ask if it was ok to walk around. It seemed better to account for the fact that I was there.

The police were ok with this, but for all they knew I could have been the killer. Anyone could.

A Deathly Still and Silence

Police foot patrols skirted the perimeter of the red light area. Squad cars circled the main drag and turned into side streets and alleys. The area was engulfed in a deathly still and silence only broken by the occasional hum of a car engine.

There was a temporary police unit set up in London Road which was close to Handford Road.

It was around 10.30pm. Apart from the police and the occasional hooded cyclist there was virtually no one else around. I didn't see any working girls that night.

It seemed to me that the policing was now at such a level that most of the surrounds were just about closed down to the normal activity that usually occurred in a time line from around 7pm till perhaps 5am.

Apart from the policing I imagined that the occasional walker who came into view may have been under cover or perhaps involved with other organisations who took it upon themselves to patrol the area.

So finally the area seemed to be under control, but I wondered if this level of surveillance wasn't too late.

As I walked around I tried to understand how these five girls had been taken from these streets, stripped, murdered and dumped off within just a few miles.

A Predator Who Knew the Girls

How was it happening? It seemed to me that whoever was taking these girls was known to them and to a certain degree would have been in their trust. When the first girl, Tania Nicol was reported missing on 30th October it may not have caused undue alarm to the other girls.

Perhaps only when Gemma Adams was reported missing on November 15th did the possibility of an abductor or something more sinister begin to register with the families, police and media.

At that stage my mind was focused on the kind of fictional stuff I was writing about. It would have been easy for a gang to take girls off the streets and hold them in some kind of compound or hideout.

There must have been a number of theories by now but I hadn't really thought that the girls had been murdered. I'm not sure how closely the police were tracking things from November 15th but I imagined that they must have stepped up things quite a bit after the disappearance of Gemma Adams.

Although the most likely scenario was that the girls were being picked up in cars from the streetside, no one really would have known if this was the case.

It was possible that arrangements for transactions could be made by mobile phone calls and perhaps the girls had gone to an address or meeting place.

I considered that CCTV footage in and around the Portman Road area and tracking of phone calls of potential suspects would form an integral part of police enquiries.

But CCTV is not always reliable, nor is it a deterrent when so many people who inhabit the streets in the twilight hours do so with the protection of hooded tops.

And so it was confirmed that the police were actually dealing with a murder, when the body of Gemma Adams was discovered on December 2nd. I wonder if surveillance was upped to another level then, as perhaps for the first time, the prospect of a serial killer loomed, with Tania Nicol still unaccounted for.

Anneli Alderton disappeared the following day. At the time I didn't realise that she was the same girl I had spent some time with months before. Then the very next day Annette Nicholls was reported missing.

Taken Under the Eyes of the Police

My thoughts were, are these girls being taken from the streets under the eyes of police and private patrols? Because surely if they were there would be witnesses that could account for something.

To cover an area like that you would need a high number of people in plain clothes, cyclists, unmarked cars and decoy hoodies etc. Additionally you would need people watching from roofs, office buildings, houses and flats, the football ground and any possible vantage point.

For all I knew this level of scanning the area may well have been in operation. It would have if I had been able to advise.

On December 8th came the tragic but almost expected news that the body of Tania Nicol had been found by police divers at Copdock Mill. To my mind this was confirmation of a serial killer.

Once more than one girl was reported missing, I think most people feared the worst. The fact that two bodies were discovered in water suggested the killer or killers may have had some forensic awareness. To possibly have access and the trust of these girls led me to believe that a member of the police force or some kind of community worker could be involved. We all had our theories and my mind was focused in this direction at times.

This case was now the only thing anyone seemed to be talking about. It was almost impossible to think that someone was taking these young women from such a small area, undetected.

Killer Playing Russian Roulette

It was a unique case where the killer seemed intent on playing Russian roulette and would continue until he or she or they were caught.

By Monday 11th December yet another woman went off the radar. This time she was named as Paula Clennell. So in the space of just over a week two bodies had been discovered and there were three other young women missing.

How could Paula have disappeared? Surley by now any girl working the streets would have been tracked over every centimetre. Could it have been that none of the girls were actually taken off the streets?

After my 45 minute walk I returned to the car. I drove off in the direction of Levington to see what the area looked like. Of all the scenes I saw around that time nothing quite prepared me for the scene there.

A few police cars and cones seemed to be caught in a time freeze and I sensed a death feel in the night air.

I arrived home around midnight and switched on the tv. The coverage of the murders seemed to be running 24/7. The next few days were spent answering the phone as the national newspapers were looking for leads and contacts. I was able to put them in touch with a few people who were close to the scene.

Working Girls in The Guardian

There were also a number of interviews conducted that appeared in the press the following day. I tended to favour The Guardian as my main point of contact.

I did a few interviews and a couple of the working girls made valuable contributions, in one case, giving an accurate timeline that seemed to differ from that released by the police regarding the last known sighting of Annette Nicholls.

There were also mobile numbers that I gave to television news crews and in all cases the girls were able to earn a fee for their commendable on-screen contributions.

Things were happening at break neck speed. I found myself co-ordinating an insight through the eyes of heroin addicts whose comments were going out to a huge audience.

Additionally I gave several statements to the police at my house. All of my walls were covered in photographs and writing from my research of the area for my books and filmscript.

It must have startled the police officers as they entered my 30 foot living room which was covered in information and images. It occurred to me that I might put myself in the frame as someone who was obsessed with the scene.

Despite this possibility I did not remove a single item from the room and was able to prove to them that I had already released a book some months before which had its heart in the streets of Ipswich.

SKY NEWS

This only proved I really was writing about things.

There was no doubt that the police were stretched to the limit trying to tie up an enormous amount of information over a short time period.

Nightclub Shoot-Out

In the middle of all this there was an unrelated murder at some kind of nightclub shoot out in Ipswich for them to contend with.

Ipswich was now engulfed by a police and media presence from all over the UK and beyond.

Some of my neighbours had already commented on the Sky News piece and they were soon to see the Sky van with it's satellite dish outside my house. It was to become a common sight over the next few days.

So much happened over the weekend of the 16th and 17th of December. A national newspaper had arrived around 11am and conducted an interview and taken photographs of me and the images that covered the walls.

Sky News phoned to ask if they could do a piece on Anneli Alderton plus some background shots of my living space.

I had told the guys at Sky that I had once dropped Ms Alderton off at an address in Colchester and they wanted to track it down and do some filming. We arranged for Sky to come and pick me up around 4 in the afternoon.

Deja Vu

As I waited for them to arrive I had some kind of deja vu experience that shook me. I was standing in my living room in the same place I had once had an in-depth conversation with Anneli.

During that conversation Anneli said something so honest and pure that it was to x-ray itself on my being. She had been talking about her time in prison and problems with drugs. Then she uttered these words, 'on top of all this I have a drink problem' - and as she spoke those words I could detect the alcohol on her breath.

Those ten words told me so much more about her as a person and I felt pity for her. She seemed to appreciate my concerns. This young lady made an impression on me and I felt sadness for her plight.

So back to the deja vu, or whatever it was that made me feel faint. Just as the Sky vehicles arrived outside I suddenly inhaled the alcoholic breath of Anneli, it was like she was there with me.

As I opened the door to the crew I quickly told them of Anneli's presence and at that moment I could forgive the guys if they thought I was losing it.

I was trying to explain things to them but they were clearly more concerned in finding the address in Colchester. So off we all went. I managed to find the road and tried to identify the house.

I had dropped Anneli off there around 3am once and I remember how she said to me 'please wait till I go in'...which I had done.

After walking up and down the road I was unable to identify the actual house, although as I was to find out a few days later, we were virtually outside it.

Despite my attempts looking for 10 minutes or so and asking a few neighbours, we had to abort the filming and I felt as though I had wasted the time of the guys from Sky. As I got back in the car I apologised but the team were ok about it and thanked me for my efforts.

Another News Crew

It must have been around 5.30 when I was dropped back off at home and within a few minutes there was a knock at the door and there stood a local television news crew to do a feature.

They had arranged to come around and in the rush of everything I had forgotten that they were coming, so it was quite lucky I had got back in time.

While they were doing an interview and some filming I realised that Channel 4 were coming to the house around 7pm and things were getting a little hectic.

As it happened a representative from Channel 4 phoned to cancel and re-arranged to meet up on the Monday, then moments after this call a press photographer phoned to ask if he could take some shots that evening...all this on a Saturday night.

As a tv crew left the house the photographer arrived with a young lady who may have been his girlfriend. He took some pictures from dramatic angles and as someone who takes an interest in photography I was very impressed with what I saw, but I never knew if they were ever published.

It must have been past 10pm when they left and I finally sunk into the sofa and tried to switch off for a while by watching Match of the Day.

By this time my 18 year old live-in daughter decided to move out for a while. The house had become something of a television studio with a constant stream of comings and goings.

There had been so much going on with people coming in and out of the house that I discovered someone's laptop in the open plan kitchen and there was a sound boom on the floor, not to mention various cables and leads in the living room.

I was eventually able to get everything back to the rightful owners after trying to work out who did what and where they did it.

Filming with Sky News

Sometime through the football I must have fallen into a deep sleep because the next thing I knew was that the telephone was going shorty after 8am and the tv was still on.

Sky News apologised for phoning so early but asked if I would be interested in doing a news piece to go out that night, to which I agreed. They were sending the guys over around 10am and they wanted to do some filming in my home and later on, some location filming in Ipswich.

A red top tabloid newspaper had arranged to visit me at 4pm and I was assured that everything should be tied up in time. We did all the filming in the house and it seemed to go well, then I was taken to Ipswich and we did some work in the red light area with police cars drifting by as we filmed.

It was done in the style of a walking interview with David Crabtree. Everything was polished off in around an hour and a half and they were ready to start the edit in the mobile suite that was parked outside of Ipswich railway station.

This meant that I was able to catch a train back to Colchester and arrive with a few minutes to spare before the next episode.

Beware the Tabloid Press

And what an episode that turned out to be. These tabloid types certainly go about their work in a very direct manner, but it took me a little while to realise what was going on.

They started off outside the house taking shots of my Toyota Celica which had, at some stage no doubt, been picked up on CCTV in various parts of Ipswich.

When they came in one of them said, 'you've got a blue car then'...I'm not even sure if I replied, it didn't seem relevant to anything at the time, and I was clearly being a little slow off the mark.

The journalist whose name I had heard of through the columns began to ask me about my interest and involvement in the Ipswich scene.

As I had done with the police, and all media, I spoke truthfully about how things had evolved over the last few years describing how, after the break up of a relationship, I found myself trawling the red light district of Ipswich.

I explained how I picked up one of the girls in a client situation and freely admitted that a sexual transaction had taken place. But I also explained how something she had said about herself interested me enough to want to write about it.

Things developed from there to the stage that I started to spend quite a lot of time with one of the other sex workers, initially as a client, but gradually as a friend who she could trust. And it was this girl who would ultimately become my key contact as I started to write a series of ambient and poetic short scenes from our experiences together.

The writing would be used for a book, filmscript and anything else that might develop from the work. I would even carefully transcript the incredible messages she would leave on my

SKY NEWS   CCTV IMAGE - SUFFOLK CONSTABULARY/CPS

telephone from call boxes at odd hours of the day and night.

How Sex Workers Live

All of the time I spent with this girl was giving me an understanding of how sex workers live and where they go to buy their drugs. I realised that I was far from alone in driving a girl to these dimly lit streets in the dead of night.

The journalist seemed very interested and just sat there soaking it all up and taking the odd note, and he may have been recording it for all I know but I saw no evidence of that.

Anyway he let me ramble on for about 20 minutes or so then suddenly asked me about my ex wife, who incidently was my common law wife, and not the person who had caused me deep trauma after a break up.

Then he started to ask me very personal things like did I have kids, which I did, although they were all grown up by now, and how my earlier break up from the mother of my children may have affected me. This went on a bit more and he began to probe into something that was very much in the past, 1991 to be exact.

After a little more of this I wondered what he was getting at and so I asked him, and his reply suggested that either he thought I might be in the frame as a suspect for the killings or he might be able to portray me as one.

This basically bought an abrupt end to the interview. I thought that something akin to a newspaper piece a few days earlier, might be on the agenda, when a certain Tom Stephens was splashed all over the press.

We hurriedly finalised things and off they went. I sat on the sofa for a while and figured how easy it was to get stitched up by these people if you are not on your guard. What I hadn't considered at that moment were all the other close ups they had photographed, not to mention my wall images.

I fell asleep shortly after and was awoken by the telephone around 10 minutes to ten on this action packed Sunday night.

BBC Radio 5 Live

There was a producer on the line asking me if I would be prepared to take part in a debate about prostitution on BBC Radio 5 Live. The programme was starting in just a few minutes and they had a number of high profile people who would be taking part.

During my short excursion into the media frenzy I have to say that I was none too impressed with the BBC. They seemed crap at organising anything. More on that later. Anyway I decided to go ahead with it although I was unsure if I could make much of a contribution.

Part of the discussion referred to something Harriet Harman had commented on about some change in prostitution laws in Sweden. It made no sense to me and just seemed to be going through the motions.

Anne Widdecombe spoke well and I hope she didn't think my 'I have more respect for prostitutes than I do for politicians' was aimed at her. I'm no great fan of the phone-in things on the radio and by 22.25 hours I was relieved of my duties.

So after a quick look at the latest news on tv I dropped off to sleep again.

An Arrest

On Monday came the dramatic news that the police had arrested Tom Stephens following the interview he had given to a Sunday newspaper in which he admitted knowing all 5 girls who had been murdered. At the time his name meant nothing to me but when I thought back he sounded like someone who I had been told about a few months earlier.

During a conversation I once had with a woman called Jacci, I'd asked her if anyone else treated the girls in the way that I did. In the case of Jacci I had once washed her hair at my Colchester home and I think she appreciated a little warmth and kindness.

Jacci had mentioned someone in particular who would spend a lot of time in the red light area either parked up in his car, offering warmth and shelter, or driving the girls off at all hours of the night to pick up their drugs.

It seemed to me that he was more or less a permanent fixture and had a closer insight to what was going on down there than anyone else, including the police and vice squad. At the time I felt a little envious as he would have far more access to the background and information than I would.

Having said that, it was doubtful he or anyone else would be compiling research for writing. Jacci may or may not have mentioned his name at the time, but from her description I was sure that the person she had spoken about was Tom Stephens.

This was later confirmed, when following his arrest, I was asked by the police if he was known to me to which I answered no. The reason the police asked me about him was because my landline telephone number had been called from his mobile on a couple of occasions.

Knowing what I did about him I was able to suggest to the police that perhaps he was even closer to the girls than I may have thought and had access to their mobile telephone contacts.

The Strange World of Tom Stephens

If he was tracking Jacci and a high number of other girls he might have taken it on himself to try and account for their movements. This did seem strange to me at the time and it does to this day.

Jacci had stayed at mine overnight and as far as I can recall she didn't make or receive any calls or text messages between around 10pm and 10am. During the time she was with me I was able to gain a valuable insight into her life and enjoyed her company.

The fact that my telephone number was on the radar of Tom Stephens made me wonder what kind of level of intelligence he had built up about the girls' movements.

As it happened I was pretty sure I hadn't spoken to him at any time and suggested to the police that he may have been checking on the whereabouts of a girl. But it did seem odd, and I seem to think one of his calls was logged in the afternoon which didn't make any sense.

If he was calling my landline, how many other numbers was he tracking? It would appear that he may have been some kind of self appointed agent who wanted to know everything he could about a girl at any given time.

Surely though, loaded with this information he would have been in a position to pass on more knowledge than just about anyone else in respect of the girls movements at those crucial times.

The arrest of Tom Stephens was bound to shed light on the case in one way or another, and I have to say, at that stage I thought the police might have their man.

He certainly fitted the profile I had in mind. Very close to the scene. Former work within the police. Access to drugs. Known to and trusted by the girls. And a few other things that were to come to light that did not make the mainstream press.

Supercharged Atmosphere

Tuesday 19th December 2006 was the most extraordinary day. Sky News had phoned quite early, around 8.30am, to ask if I would be available to do another news piece.

We arranged to meet around 10.15 in the morning by the Sky News van that was parked in London Road, an area which has been central to the red light area of Ipswich for many years.

I managed to park my car in Sainsbury's as I had done on several previous occasions. The entire area was packed with police and media. There was a crackle in the air, helicopters whirred above and the atmosphere was supercharged. It seemed like things had somehow stepped up another gear.

This was by far the most activity I had seen on these streets and I soon found out why. Suddenly I was surrounded by reporters, some of them representing the German and Swedish press, there must have been at least 40 of them around me. It had just been announced that the police had made another arrest from a house in London Road, literally 50 yards or so from where we were standing.

I was asked if I had heard of a David Welton, this name meant nothing to me but it was the one being mentioned for an hour or so by some of the reporters. They had established that an early morning raid at 79 London Road resulted in a second arrest to go with that of Tom Stephens.

Walking Interview with Jeremy Thompson

The news piece that had been planned was for Jeremy Thompson to do a walking interview with me around the London Road area. Jeremy opens with 'I'm surprised in a way that you're not a suspect' and my answer mentions the national newspaper who had hinted that they thought I might be involved in some way. As we are walking we are being watched by all the other media, police and bystanders who were standing pretty much in silence.

We speak about the first police arrest of Tom Stephens and I express how his profile and behaviour had made his arrest inevitable. Jeremy asks me if I think that the girls who had lost their lives would have known their killer beforehand. I was glad he asked me this because I was able to answer in such a way that

I had been convinced all along that the killer would have been known to them.

I felt the killer had their trust. There were links between the girls and my assumption was that the killer was close at hand.

It was an opportunity to say something that I felt sure of - that the police would have had eye to eye contact with the killer and that surviving women would have had eye to eye contact with him.

We talk about what these streets are like at 2am, and I describe them as a kind of misty and murky netherland where sometimes you see only shadows disappearing round corners and into doorways, and how something about the place can cling to your skin.

It offered a chance to somehow express an almost poetic backdrop to the area, the type of stuff I had been writing about, and how, incredibly, I had become almost addicted to these streets in my search to write about their twilight inhabitants.

I really appreciated the questions I was being asked and towards the close of the piece I was given the opportunity to say some-thing for the girls, their friends and their families that I hoped would connect with them and the public.

"These Girls Came into the World as Angels"

These are the words that I said...' These girls came into the world as angels and they have left as angels - whatever happened in their lives I have so much respect for them'.

You can spend a lot of time writing poetry about working girls and their lives but my books had only a limited audience and somehow it meant a lot personally to be allowed to express something I felt so strongly about to a potentially massive television audience in the UK and beyond.

Perhaps I wanted to put myself in the media spotlight for a while as some kind of self appointed voice to speak up for these women.

Some of the things I had witnessed over a couple of years had changed my life and I wanted to try and get a message across to the public that these girls were tragic victims, despite the fact that at some stage many of them had got themselves into a world that would crush them bit by bit.

After we finished I shook hands with Jeremy Thompson and I was really grateful that he had conducted the interview in such a sensitive manner.

At the time I hadn't realised that the word 'angels' used in this context had registered with anyone, but some years later I discovered that it had.

Sky had said it was ok for me to speak to other media and for a while I was engulfed. I can't even remember how many interviews I did or who they were all with, but I think they included the BBC, The Press Association, a German magazine and Channel 4.

After about 40 minutes of this I accepted the offer of a coffee with a Sky News producer and we made our way to Sainsbury's.

As we were walking back we were being followed by reporters and television crews, and I was wondering why they were taking such an interest in me.

SKY NEWS

Cameraman Falls Down Grass Bank

We walked along a path which had a grass bank to the side and in these moments of high drama something funny happened but it didn't seem right to laugh. A cameraman filming us from the grass bank tripped over a wire or something and tumbled down the other side and out of view.

Such was the mayhem that no one took the slightest bit of notice and we continued the short walk. We made it to Sainsbury's and so did quite a few of those who were following us. We managed to get a table and sat down with the coffees.

Reporters and press people sat nearby and seemed to be listening in, but the conversation centred around the production guy as I was interested in learning how he had moved into media after graduating in history.

I appreciated the 20 minute break and felt that after a non stop morning I should return home and follow the news on television. Although I was at the front end of a lot of the stuff that was going down, it helped to see it all put together on the news.

Just after 1pm I drove back to my home in Colchester and got back in half an hour or so. I switched onto Sky News and they were reporting the early morning arrest that had taken place at around 5am in London Road.

The name of the person who they taken into custody was different from the person who had been mentioned earlier that morning. The second arrest would be named as Steve Wright and I assumed that 79 London Road may well have been a property that had been converted into flats.

BBC News 24 and the Crazy Taxi Journey

As I attempted to get something to eat there a spate of telephone calls on my landline and I was asked if I would be able to return to Ipswich around 5 in the afternoon to do a news piece for BBC News 24. The BBC producer, calling from a mobile from somewhere in Ipswich presumably, said they would send a car for me at around 4ish. Other phone calls followed including one from Channel 4 news who also wanted to put something out.

I told them about the BBC News 24 thing and I think they said they would arrange something later. In between all of this I managed to do several telephone interviews with the national press.

Some people with knowledge of the area were reluctant to speak to the media, although a few of the girls had come forward and spoken openly and honestly about the area and their lives.

The media were hungry for any angle they could get and I wondered how the BBC thing might pan out.

Well, the first part didn't turn out too well as the car that had been sent to pick me up arrived 40 minutes late, which was going to make things tight if they wanted something to be filmed around 6.30 as they had mentioned.

What happened following the car arriving at my house was a bit of a haze then and it is now, more than three years later, but I will try and get this incredible series of events in the order they happened.

The driver said we were going to Suffolk Police HQ in Martlesham Heath to meet people from the BBC. I thought this strange as everyone else had been located in London Road after the second arrest.

He drove fast, it was foggy, and as we sped along the A12 I had a feeling that we were going to the wrong place and wondered if the message from the producer to the Ipswich taxi firm had somehow got lost in translation.

When we got nearer Martlesham we seemed to take some short cuts, the driver was going faster than the speed limit, and at one time we jumped some lights and went across a grass verge. It was a good job I had my seat belt on.

After our arrival I got out of the car and made for the BBC van that I quickly found, there were about 3 of them there including Jon Sopel who had his feet up and appeared to be taking a nap in the vehicle.

I introduced myself to what I assumed to be a producer and he had no knowledge of anything that had been planned. After a quick phone call he confirmed what I had been thinking during the manic taxi journey and said he would order a taxi to take me to London Road.

At least I managed to exchange a few sentences with Mr Sopel but I got the impression my arrival may have disturbed him and he wore the expression of a stern schoolmaster.

Police Officers Walking Towards Me

So I was just standing about by their van when I noticed these two police officers walking quickly towards me. At the same time these two gentlemen were walking my way I noticed how deserted the site was. It had been crawling with production people during my other visits.

They asked me who I was and what I was doing on site and I told them that I was waiting for a taxi the beeb had ordered to take me to London Road to do something for the news.

It was clear there was something wrong but I had no idea what it was. Nothing was explained and I don't remember if I asked. It was quite worrying as I felt that it was something that I may have said or done over the last few days.

Anyway, I was allowed to wait near the main gate for the car to arrive but I had an officer either side of me. I saw Martin Brunt walk by and he looked confused, it must have looked like I was under some kind of arrest.

After 20 minutes or so the taxi arrived. I got in the thing and was quite relieved to get away from there.

We got to London Road in around 15 minutes but by now it was about quarter past seven. At least the guys there had been expecting me and I tried to explain what had been going on in the last couple of hours.

Vapour Puffs in the Night Air

I don't think these kind of people were much interested in what had happened as they were rightly focused on doing news. Anyway, after a few minutes I was introduced to Sangita Myska who was much more welcoming than her colleague back at Martlesham.

So we did a piece and I thought it went well, but as far as I could make out it was never broadcast.

Thinking about it, I wondered if the stuff I did for BBC television, about 3 or 4 interviews was held back for any reason. Everything else I had got involved with for tv, radio and press had been used and some of it was repeated through the night on news loops.

It was now past 8 o'clock and it was freezing cold. Sangita shivered beside me and when we spoke our breath made little vapour puffs in the night air.

After a while I was informed that they would order a taxi to take me home and was able to wait in the warmth of one of their vans.

So yet another taxi journey, but this one travelled at far more acceptable speeds and I must have arrived home at about 9ish.

The day's events had given me a lot to think about. I followed it all up as best I could by switching from channel to channel and was able to watch the piece I did for Sky News earlier that morning several times, as it was repeated hourly through the night.

It had come out really well, and it occurred to me that I had never really seen anything quite like it before. After looking on BBC News 24 I was unable to find the interview we did, so unless it had gone out earlier it must have been canned.

I reflected on what had happened at police HQ, and why, after offering so much assistance to the police and media, I had been treated in such a way.

Wednesday arrived and I fired off an email to Martin Brunt to try and explain the previous night's events. We had been in touch on a number of occasions over the last few days, some by telephone and with emails too as we shared information and ideas on the case.

I also phoned the BBC to ask what had happened at Martlesham Heath as I should never have been there in the first place. Eventually, after being passed on to about 5 different people I got an answer which went something like this...'sorry, we can't tell you what happened last night'.

Wire Taps?

Later that day I got an explanation of the police stuff, but not from anyone connected to the BBC. When I fully understood the circumstances of the limit on my movements by the police I was relieved to find that it was nothing to do with me personally.

The reason that I had been monitored and escorted away from police HQ was apparently due to an alleged incident of some kind of wire tapping.

It was explained to me that certain members of a news organisation had gained access to the police canteen and assembled listening devices under the tables and were then able to eavesdrop on police conversations that could have been very revealing.

There had been a stream of on-going police press conferences that would give carefully considered information that was shared by everyone on an equal basis, but it was clear that some members of the media were looking for something more.

On one particular occasion, and within seconds of the conclusion of a Suffolk Police style 'breaking news' release, I spotted Martin Brunt in the corner of my television screen as he made a call on his mobile, a couple of seconds later my phone rang...I was almost able to see Martin for a few seconds while we spoke.

Steve Wright - Suspect with a Capital 'S'

The call was along the lines that of the two suspects, Tom Stephens and Steve Wright, it was felt down there that the word 'suspect' had a lower case 's' in the case of Stephens, but a capital 'S' in regard to the 'more significant' detainment of Wright.

If one or both of these men were to be charged it would have been in keeping with my firm belief that the killer was close to and known to the girls, and literally living in the middle of the red light area, but in the case of Wright, it was closer than I had expected.

There were more telephone calls during the day, the main question being did I know Steve Wright or anything about him. He was unknown to me but over the next few hours the press were unravelling information about him from a number of sources.

On Friday December 21st Steve Wright was charged with the murder of the five girls. I will never forget how deeply respectful Detective Chief Superintendent Stewart Gull was as he read out their names at the hushed press conference.

He uttered each syllable slowly and carefully.

From the moment of this announcement there was a media blackout and all reporting on the murders and on Stephen Wright was suspended.

The phone calls stopped, and everything went quite. With just a few days to go before Christmas I was able to think about organising some cards and presents for my daughters and close family.

Relieved of my Duties

It felt like I had been relieved of my duties along with hundreds of others after an intense period of all kinds of experiences and activity that were a one off in anyone's lifetime.

Although things had quietened down on the reporting front there was still a very strange experience to follow.

A few days later I was coming back home from town and saw a member of the clergy who was walking up the slope that leads out of my estate. He was dressed in a purple robe, and to this day I have been unable to identify his status within the church.

He seemed very senior and my guess was that he may have been a Bishop. There is a church and a vicarage nearby. I'd only had the odd sighting of the local vicars during the years I have lived here, and from what I remember they all wore black.

I'm not sure what prompted me but as we were about to pass I stopped to ask him something that had been playing on my mind regarding the deja vu thing I had about Anneli Alderton.

I asked him point blank if he had any idea as to how a deja vu with scent as it's base could be explained in a human or religious way.

The amazing thing was that with each word that I uttered the sound seemed to travel on for miles. It was the purest sound of my voice or any voice I had ever heard.

I was actually looking past him and across into the distance and could see these houses reflecting the sunlight about 2 miles away. At that moment I was convinced that anyone in those houses and beyond could hear what I was saying.

Then something else occurred to me, I was looking in the direction of the resting place of Anneli.

He didn't offer any explanation, and off he went. Sometimes I wonder if the conversation ever took place. It was surreal, almost beyond anything in a dream.

Voices

Miss D

One of me mates put me on to this bloke who was fuckin loaded. He lived in a mansion. It had big gates and a drive and was all floodlit. We better call 'im Giles, yeah that will do, 'cause I don't mind you recording this but I aint gonna name no cunt.

Don't worry, I change all the names anyway...I'm calling you Leanne for the purpose of this.

I like that name meself, thanks, perhaps I'll use it.

(we both laugh).

Anyway, I used to get a lift there from a mate 'cause I knew I'd get enough money from the job ta let Dan have £40. Giles used to 'ave a room with all this fucking shit in. Shackles the lot. I would dress 'im up in all this rubber gear with a mask and sometimes a german war helmet or somethin'. Then I'd slash the cunt across his shoulders with a Stanley knife. He used to scream out in pain. Sometimes the blood would get on me.

Fucking hell.

Yeah, anyway he liked to be left hanging there on the wall for an hour. I used ta go an' watch his telly in a big fuck off room, 'an put me feet up...there was coke, drink, fuckin' anythin' you wanted.

You should have moved in.

Yeah, I fuckin' shoulda. He used ta pay £300 in twenty pound notes. They were always brand new.

What about the sex?

"He Never Touched Me"

He used to wank himself off afterwards. He never touched me. Not ever.

Tell me about Laura, is it true?

You heard about that...yeah, it's true.

Please run through it for the purpose of this interview.

Can I smoke?

Yes, I'll get you an ashtray.

Laura had a regular client called Steve, he was in love with her...he was obsessed...he'd bring her food at 1.30am when she was still on the beat...sometimes he would wait for hours in his car by the BMW place...Laura told me how he had taken her into town one day and bought loads of clothes for her on his credit card...I suppose they were a kind of couple in a way.

Well, they used to hold hands if that is anything to go by. Steve used to take her to get her drugs at all hours of the day and night...he was always on call...so I don't reckon that he had a job, but he had fucking loads of money.

I think his mother died and he went to Wales or somewhere for a couple of days. Anyway, I remember Laura telling me that he had given her a spare key to the house while he was away. She used to stay there the odd night, but most of the time she would be at Leroy's in town. She used to get it on with Leroy.

Anyway when Steve came back to the house she and Leroy and some of his mates had taken all the furniture, the widescreen, hi fi, the whole fucking lot. Anything that had a sell on value had gone. They even emptied out the garage. They took Steve's other car and moved a lot of the gear in that. Think they set fire to it...not to hide anything, just for the buzz...

"She'd Fucking Ripped Him Off and he Still Wanted Her"

Even after this had happened, Steve came down one night and tried to talk to Laura, he didn't seem that bothered, it was so strange...she'd fucking ripped him off and he still wanted her...

Laura was just numb to it all by then. She was glazed. She got done for shop lifting just after all that happened, I don't think Steve even reported what she'd done to the police.

There was one punter, he used to turn up with a toddler asleep in the baby seat. I saw him for about 3 months. We did business with the kid snoring away in the back of the car. Little boy it was. I asked him how he happened to be driving around with the kid asleep like that and he said that it was the only way they could get him off to sleep at night.

I think it was the punter's wife who had the idea about taking the little boy out for a drive at night to get him off to sleep. I must have seen this bloke a dozen or so times. The kid slept through all of it. Mainly gave the guy blow jobs.

I used to see this posh bloke, he lived in one of them executive house things in Woodbridge. Never knew what he did for a living. He could 'ave been a bank manager or solicitor or summit, he was a regular for about a year or so, then 'e just never turned up any more. I used to go to his house and we would do business in a games room.

He had this thing about fucking me over the snooker table. He always paid over the going rate. Gave me an extra 20 quid and always offered to make me a tea or coffee or something.

"His Wife Was Lovely Looking and the Kids as Well"

One night I stayed a bit longer and he showed me around the house, I saw a picture of his wife and kids. His wife was lovely looking and the kids as well. He had 2 boys and a girl, and I asked if they were still married.

For all I knew they could have still been living there. He told me that they were separated. His wife had left him for the builder who had done the games room extension. When I think about it maybe that was some kinda way of gettin' back at 'er.

The Kosovans, Albanians an that. They are more likely to knock you about than our lot. I have been punched, kicked and head butted by those cunts. One pushed me out of the car one night in the middle of fucking nowhere. Had to walk for an hour before I saw a road sign. Me mouth bleeding and me head pounding.

Did you tell the police?

Na, never told 'em.

Miss K

The first night I went out I was shaking. I had been thinking about it for months. My friend Kelly had been doing it for ages, I think it was her that finally talked me into it. I was in debt. I just had no way of paying the bills and the cards. I used to do drugs but I was not dependent on them, it was only after a few months that I realised that I was getting hooked on it. I managed to pay off some of what I owed, then things just seemed to change.

What changed.

"It's So Easy to Become Someone Else"

Well, owing money, I thought why bother paying it. It's so easy to become someone else. The other girls taught me how you can reinvent yourself. New name, just walk away from the rented flat, I soon had about 10 different places to crash. No need to worry about doing a job. All the jobs I did were shit anyway. I remember Kelly asking me what I earned when I was doing all these

casual jobs and I told her that I used to clear about £175 a week
if I was lucky. She said that I could earn that in one night and
have the rest of the week to myself.

Yeah, there are some shit jobs out there.

You're telling me, I've done enough of them since I left uni.

Uni, I didn't realise you did uni, where were you?

I was at Essex.

What, just down the road from here?

Yeah, did Computer Science.

*You seem quite together to me, a lot of the girls that I have
interviewed are entirely dependent on drugs.*

Yeah, I'm just holding it together.

But, surely you want to break away from it.

Of course, but I'm not sure when.

Would you like some coffee?

Yes please, white, two and a half sugars.

You are really polite.

My parents bought me up well, they don't know about any of
this.

Miss J

Where did you spend last Christmas?

Peterborough Prison.

Christ, how come?

Shop lifting...I knew that if I got caught around that time that
I'd get about 6 weeks, and if I didn't get caught I could sell
some of the stuff for gear.

What was it like?

It was ok, they'd just built on a new wing and it was
comfortable...better than where I was staying.

*So in a way you were actually pleased to have somewhere to 'stay'
over Christmas.*

Yeah.

And you have no stigma about it at all.

None.

Thanks for agreeing to do this.

It's ok, you got a drink or something?

Like what, tea or coffee?

No, like vodka or summit.

I don't drink, but someone left some gin here the other week, there's a bit of that.

Top.

I'll get it...

Thanks, can I have a cold drink as well?

Yeah, I've got some tropical juice.

(She is drinking the gin straight and nods a yes).

Christ, have you drunk that already, there were about 10 measures there.

Yeah, thas nuffin.

"Got a Habit, Had to Feed the Habit"

How old are you?

24.

How long have you been doing this?

Six years.

How did it start?

Same as most girls, got a habit, had to feed the habit.

How much does your habit cost you?

Dunno, exactly cos I support me boyfriend as well but I reckon I do about £80 a day on gear fer meself.

Eighty quid a day, what every day?

Yeah, pretty much.

What are you on?

Heroin.

You girls are so honest, you never hide anything from me.

No need to hide anyfin.

Do you know Stacey from Birmingham?

Yeah, we used to share a room down London Road.

Stacey told me so much about her life.

Stacey is a really lovely person, she lost her kids, they went into care.

I wrote stuff about her, poetry of a kind.

Was that you did that, oh, wow that was beautiful, she showed me.

That's nice to hear.

Some of the punters treat us nice, you're nice.

I wish I could save you all.

We 'ave to save ourselves.

Yeah, I know, but at least when you are here I can offer some kind of warmth and kindness, even if it's only for an hour or so.

We do appreciate it, just not very good at showing it.

Miss L

Where are you from originally?

Felixstowe.

Quite local then.

Quite, we moved to Ipswich when I was 10.

When you say we, who exactly?

My mum and dad and sister.

Would you say you came from a stable background?

Pretty much yeah, we was just an ordinary family.

Are your parents still together...married?

They separated when I was 16.

So did they get divorced?

They did but not for a few years.

Would you say that your mum and dad splitting up affected you?

No more than it affected my sister or most of my friends who had been through the same kind of thing.

I suppose I'm trying to establish if anything in your past, your family for instance may have led in any way to how you live now

I'm not sure if any of that made any difference, I still saw my dad and being 16 I was out with my mates most of the time.

Did your mum remarry?

Well, good as, this David bloke moved in with us.

And is he still with your mum?

He was around for a few years but he went off and we never heard from him again.

Did you get on with him?

He was ok with me and sis.

"I Wanted to be a Hairdresser"

How was your schooling?

I did ok but was happy to leave.

What did you want to do when you left school?

I wanted to be a hairdresser.

Did that happen?

It happened until I blew it.

OK, so I am guessing that what you do now led to that.

It did, but from starting on the drugs to getting the sack must have bin about a year.

So, basically then, you had a fairly normal upbringing and education, got into a profession - I'm talking the hairdressing one, that you were happy to do and at some stage when you started to take drugs things went downhill.

I was smoking weed when I was 13 but then so was everyone else, took cocaine when I was 15 or 16, but nothing really affected me much until I took heroin.

How old were you when you took heroin?

19.

Who introduced it to you?

Some guy I had met.

Met where?

"It was Dead Easy to get Anything you Wanted"

There was a load of us that used ta hang out together, parties
'an that.

Was it your free choice to take it?

Yeah, it was, in fact I asked if I could try it 'an some of 'em
said don't do it, but that's history now.

So it was your own free will.

Totally.

You hear of people, girls getting groomed into it.

It can happen but I don't really know anyone it's 'appened to,
well they aint said.

Is this the kind of thing you might discuss with the other girls?

How do you mean?

Well, how drugs came into their lives.

We 'ave spoken about it sometimes yeah...and maybe sum of 'em
were kind of led into it by their partners....but, I don't fink
they were forced into it, it just happens around you.

So, your friends and the people who were around could quite easily get hold of drugs in this town.

It was dead easy to get anything you wanted.

Is there anything that you regret?

I regret I am not a mother to my little girl, I fucking regret that.

I'm sorry, I didn't know that. Only talk about it if you can.

"I Try and Block it Out"

She's with me every waking second. I dream of her. She's sleeping on my shoulder. I hear her breathing.

They took her. Said it would be for the best.

Are you ok?

I try and block it out. The drugs...use them as a barrier...but there ain't no drugs can block out that kind of pain. Death would block it out. Nothing else...just death.

Shall we stop for a while?

No, it can't make it any worse.

When did this happen?

Two years ago.

How old is she?

She'll be 4 on September 2nd.

Her name?

Faith.

That's a nice name.

It was my Great Grandmother's name. I never knew her...she looked like a 20's filmstar...kept her picture in a locket, but I lost it...just like I lost everything else.

Do you have any access to Faith?

"I Blow Her a Kiss 'Cause I Can't Hold Her"

I'm not allowed as things stand...but I see her sometimes, at the little nursery she goes to...I watch from the fence...the people at the school...they don't know me...they don't know I stand there sometimes. I blow my daughter a kiss...I blow her a kiss 'cause I can't hold her...she's looked in my eyes, and that's the only thing that makes me cry...nothing else affects me like she does...nothing.

Other girls, other girls who work down there, I've heard they've lost their children too.

I can think of quite a few who have, yeah...and it's our own fault...I know it's my fault.

I see a point in your lives where it all turns.

It's when you can't live without Heroin. It's when Heroin takes over your life.

"Some of their Own Doctors are Junkies"

Everything. It can happen to anyone...don't matter where you come from, rich, poor, good or evil...I've seen 'em in mansions and I've seen 'em in squats...and some of 'em don't even have a squat...after a while you can spot one a mile off, but the public, a lot of the time they would have no idea. They would never fucking believe that some of their own doctors are junkies. There's policemen, firemen...paramedics on the gear...

What, on duty?

On duty 'n off fucking duty - 'an there's well known people in
this town who preach about this and fucking preach about that but
us girls know that they are addicts just like us, 'an yet they
are better at hiding it, 'an they got the fucking money to pay
for it.

You must see so much.

I see what's going down. There's two worlds living side by side.
But the world thas' growin' fastest is the world that I know,
'cause there's more and more people getting hooked on somefin
than there ever was. There's skunk around now that fucks people's
minds up 'cause it's different than the weed that was on the
streets only a couple of years ago.

In what way is it different?

It's about 10 times stronger than those piss leaves that people
used to puff on...there's people growing it at home, in their
lofts, on farms, right little drug factories, even hidden from
the heat seeking gear on the police helicopters. I know 'cause I
seen some of 'em. It's business and they make far more profit
than the corner shop, and they don't have the bovver of keeping
books like my Dad had to 'cause it's all cash and only they know
what they are making.

Are there any around here?

The ones I seen are about 20 minutes out of town.

What driving?

In a car, yeah.

Miss R

Give me a rough idea of your day, how and when it starts and what happens.

When it starts...well I suppose it starts when I wake up.

What time do you wake up?

Well, just lately, I wake up 'bout 5 o'clock.

What, morning or night?

Oh, that a be five in the evenin'.

Right, so you get up about 5ish, then what?

I 'ave a couple of cups of coffee, a bit of a smoke, 'an watch a bit of telly for half hour or so, 'an get a bit of breakfast...

Breakfast at half past five in the evening.

Yeah, hadn't thought of it like that, but I 'ave a bit of toast 'an cereal 'an whatever.

Where are you living?

Well, at the moment I'm staying in a flat that one of the other girls is sort of babysitting or somfin'.

Babysitting a flat?

Yeah, Kelly said to me that she 'ad this one bedroomed flat for 6 weeks or so while the bloke she knows is away and that there was a sofa to sleep on in the livin' room if I wanted.

That sounds like a useful arrangement then. Rent free I take it.

Rent free yeah.

And bill free too?

"I Need to Find 'Bout 80 Quid a Day for the Gear"

I ain't paid no bills for two years, apart from a couple of fines, and I never paid them, someone else give me the money.

So you have virtually no financial outgoings then like most people would have.

Well you could say that or you could say that my financial outgoins is a lot more that 'uver people 'cause I need to find 'bout £80 quid a day for the gear.

By gear you mean the drugs.

Yeah.

OK, so you get up around 5 in the evening at the moment, get a bit of breakfast and so on and then what?

Well, I 'ave a shower, do me hair...and that kind of thing. Then I get ready 'an that.

What about your flat mate Kelly?

Well sometimes she's there 'an sometimes she aint. If she's there she's most probably in 'er room 'an that.

So what time do you leave to 'go to work' as it were, and how do you get down there?

Different times, but maybe get a bus 'an get down there about half past seven or eight.

You get a bus to work.

Yeah, but I ain't never come back on one.

So, how long are you down there then and what kind of money can you expect to get on average?

Well just lately I bin working till 'bout 3 'an maybe picking up somefin like one twenie ta one eighty...an sometimes I can do two fifty.

How many nights a week are you working?

Five or six, 'an I fink seven the other week.

"It Works Out at Over Fifty Thousand a Year"

Right, so let's say at five nights a week at something like £140 a night - I'm averaging it out a little, you are picking up around £700 a week...and it's tax free of course, and that would equate to a decent salary if you were to work it out.

Well I aint never really thought of it like that, but me mate said it works out at over fifty thousand a year if it was a proppa job 'an that does sound like a lot when you put it that way.

But in a proper job you would get holidays and such, but as I understand it, you might be working 52 weeks a year.

Yeah, every week, never really thought about no holiday.

When did you last go on a holiday?

I ain't never bin on no holiday.

Not even when you were little?

Well, I ain't never bin abroad or nuffin if tha's what you mean, but I did go to Cornwall once when I was about 12 with me friend 'an her mum and it was really good. We rode on these ponies. They was bewtiful. I liked that. Funny, I aint neva thought of that in years.

Maybe you'll go back one day.

Yeah, maybe.

Perhaps you'll take your own children there.

Don't seem much chance of that.

So, you're working from around eight till three then. What do you do for food say?

I get stuff from the garage...coffee, chocolate...then sometimes I get taken to MacDonalds by some of the punters.

Some of the punters take you to MacDonalds?

Or Kentucky Fried Chicken or a burger bar.

How many of them do this?

Well there's a couple of them that do.

So some of the punters treat you ok then.

"They Can Knock you About a Bit"

Some of 'um do yeah...but there's a few that don't.

How many don't?

Some of the Kosovans don't. They're rude 'an some of 'em can turn nasty.

Nasty?

They can knock you about a bit.

Has this happened to you?

It's 'appened to me 'an it's 'appened to a lot of the girls.

Like what?

I've bin punched, kicked....'ad me clothes ripped 'an that.

Is this something you could tell the police about?

I could tell 'em but I aint neva bovered.

How do you get on with the police doing what you do?

Police is ok - just doing their job 'an we get cautioned sumtimes.

Do you feel in danger doing what you do?

I bin beatin up about 3 times in 4 years so I suppose doin' what I do you 'ave to expect it a bit...but apart from that I don't really feel that I'm in danger no.

I take it some of the other girls may have been beaten up too at times.

Yeah, an a lot worse than me sum of 'em.

What drugs do you take?

Heroin.

How long have you been taking it?

Since about 4 years ago.

Do you see a way out of this? Do you see a different future?

Not at the moment I don't.

Do you hope for a different future?

Yeah, suppose so.

How many other girls are working down here on the streets of Ipswich?

I would say maybe 30 regulars and perhaps another 20 or 30 who do it from time to time.

How many of them do you speak to?

"Me and Kelly Share our Coats"

I speak to most of 'em at some time or uvva but I only really know about five of 'em really well.

How well?

Well enuff to live with 'em sumtimes 'an share cloves 'an that.

You share each other clothes?

Me and Kelly share our coats.

That's a nice coat..is it yours?

No, this is one of Kelly's.

That looks expensive.

Yeah, it is. Kelly bought this one in town...fink it was about two hundred.

I heard some of you girls get your clothes by shoplifting.

Some of us 'ave nicked stuff from shops 'an sumtimes we buy it, and sumtimes a punta might buy you stuff.

Punters would buy you clothes.

The odd one, yeah.

Do some of the girls have relationships with punters?

Some do, yeah.

Anyone you know?

Several.

"The Girl Becomes the Wage Earner"

Do any of the relationships develop into something that works as a kind of sex worker / pimp partnership?

A few have I think, because sometimes a girl will be paying for a partner's drugs as well as her own, and since some of these

partners are just on benefits or summit then it's like the girl becomes the wage earner for the two of 'em.

So needs to earn double?

Well not really double, cos the more you buy the less it costs and it don't always make a lot of difference.

Have you been in a similar relationship to this?

Yeah, got the tee-shirt, but 'e wen inside for nicking cars and breakins.

Are you in any form of relationship now?

Not really, apart from one of the punters who is on my case, well, he's on the case of a lot of the girls, but he is often on the scene and I see something of him most nights.

Like what?

He'll run me 'round for drugs, take me home, tries to stay some nights, and he has, but I tend to try and keep out the way when I can cos I don't feel like I wanna take it any further than that.

Does he have a job?

Yeah, as far as I know he works shifts in a supamarket or garage.

Is he married?

He has been I think but now he lives on his own a bit out of town.

Do other punters try to see you - say in a date?

Some ask me out yeah...but I just don't really see myself sitting in a restaurant or at the pictures, it seems too far removed from where I'm at.

Do you miss that kind of lifestyle?

I don't really miss it as I neva really knew it, or if I did it was over in a flash.

How old are you?

Twenty four and hoping to make twenty five but if I don't it won't matter much to anyone.

You feel like that.

Sometimes I do yeah.

"Most of Them are Between 20 and 35"

Do you feel that by living this alternative lifestyle you are missing out on something?

I used ta, but you become removed from it and the only contact you have is by watching people out shopping on a Saturday or something and I can't say I envy them that much. My sister is living a so called normal life, but if a normal life is being in debt and being married to a jerk then I aint that bovered.

Anyone looking at you from the other side of this table might think that you earn a living as a model of some kind, how do you explain that after the lifestyle you describe.

Dunno, lucky suppose...maybe good genes.

Someone from a vice squad I once spoke to in the midlands reckoned he could more or less tell how old a working girl was and how long she had been on the gear, and what she was taking, just by looking at her for about 5 seconds. He'd seen hundreds of girls over around 10 years.

I've 'eard that...'an could probably work it out for meself if I 'ad to, but I more or less know the ages of the girls and stuff about 'em anyway.

What are the age ranges down here?

Most of them are between 20 and 35...sometimes there are a few younger ones and there's some in their 40's.

Where do they come from, are they mainly from Ipswich?

Most of them are from the Ipswich area and just outside and there's a few from Felixstowe and Colchester. Some of the girls have moved down here from up North for whatever reason, like Manchester 'an round there.

Are there ever any problems between the girls?

I aint really had no problems with any but some of the other girls have.

Like what?

"Two of the Girls Were Fighting"

Two of the girls were fighting in the middle of the road one night, kicking and punching fuck out of each uvver 'an the stuff out their bags - the money 'an that was all spilled out everywhere, the cars and the punters was driving 'round them and one of their mobiles got crushed under a wheel. The police come and it's a good job they did cos it looked like one of 'em might end up dead - as it was they had to call an ambulance for the pair of 'em.

Did they manage to pick up their stuff?

Some of it by the looks of fings but there was probably a few £10 and £20 notes blowing about near the BMW garage and I think one of the dealers was picking some of it up.

A dealer?

Well a dealer or one of their partners.

Could you tell the difference?

Sometimes I could.

So there were partners and dealers out there too some nights.

Sometimes the dealers would be parked up around there waiting for the girls to get the money so they could serve up fast as.

Did you ever buy from anyone that close by?

I have done but not often.

Who did you buy your drugs from - don't name anyone, just give me an idea.

I've got my stuff from a whole load of different dealers over the last few years.

How far would you have to go to get the drugs?

Between a few minutes walk to ten minutes in a car usually.

"Watching Out for Money More Like"

Are there a lot of dealers out there?

Plenty enuff.

So, I'm getting a picture of a possible scene down there where there are working girls, some of their partners parked up in cars, the occasional dealer floating around and the odd police car circling the area, is that a fair description?

Pretty much yeah...'an the vice squad, and a few walkers.

Oh yeah, I forgot the vice squad...who are the walkers?

Well, I describe them as sightsee'ers, some blokes just trek about watching what's going on.

Like me, I've done that.

Maybe I seen yer, but I don't remember.

I noticed a few on bikes too, are they sightsee'ers?

Some of 'em maybe 'an some of 'em are the girls partners.

Watching out for them you mean.

Watching out for the money more like.

OK, so when the girls came back from doing business they might hand the cash over to a partner.

I nevva did but some of the girls would.

Right, so let's move on to the clients...give me an idea of the kind of men who you meet through your work.

Every kind. Boy racers, shift workers, loners, professional types, single blokes, married men...I don't think there's any type of male that's excluded and some people would be shocked 'cause we have even seen men of the church and so called protectors of us workin' girls and everythin'.

Men of the church?

"A Right Little Sex Den it Was"

Yeah, I saw one regular for months and we used ta go to the church and we would do pretty much everythin', everywhere in the place. A right little sex den it was. He would always have 'is gown 'n colla on or whatever you call it and 'e was some kind of sex addict.

That would have looked good in the papers.

There was a lot of stuff that woulda looked good in the papers.

But you girls would never be in the business of exposing any type of client would you.

No, but we 'ave spoken about it at times.

Give me some examples if you can of the type of places you might go to do business.

Industrial estates mostly, that is, unless they take you to their homes or where they work.

You must have seen some very different homes then.

Yeah, from dingy little flats, caravans, lock-ups and sheds to country houses and penthouse apartments.

And office buildings?

Some office buildings, which makes yer wonder what CCTV is all about - not that it bovvers meself.

Yeah, CCTV...does it work?

"Banging on the Windscreen"

Even if it does it aint up to much.

Have you ever been caught in the act as it were?

There use ta be this bloke who went round on a moped following the punters after they picked up a girl. He would suddenly spring out of fucking nowhere banging on the windscreen or sumfin when we were parked up and doing business. He would scare the shit out of some of the blokes 'cause 'e was saying 'e was gonna report us and had taken the number plate 'an evrythin.

Did you catch a view of him?

I caught 'is face a few times, right nerdy do gooder, looked 'bout 35...'e was fuckin' strange.

So he wasn't a dogger then, given that he wasn't interrupting things.

I dunno what he was or what 'appened to 'im, maybe a punter got out the car one night and smacked him one, he was fucking asking for it.

That must have been off putting for some of your clients having someone jump them like that.

It was, specially for the married ones who thought they were gonna be rumbled.

Did that ever happen then?

"That Could Be Big Business"

I nevva heard of it but 'e could easily 'ave followed some of the blokes home.

Thinking about it, he could have blackmailed them.

He could. That could be big business.

Better still if he had hidden up once he had parked his moped, taken the numbers and followed them back somehow.

Corr yeah, see what yer mean.

Of all the guys you must meet doing this, if meet is the right word, do any of them make the kind of impression on you that makes you wish you knew them under different circumstances?

To be honest my only interest in them is to get their money, there's little things you might remember about some of them but my life is about getting from one day to the next the easiest way possible and it's easier to be free of a lot of the stuff that it might lead to.

When you say 'stuff it might lead to' what stuff?

Well, if a guy just wants to talk a while after and take me to get drugs thas' ok, but some of them talk about wanting to save me and all that 'an although sum of 'em probably really mean well it's easier for me not to go down that road.

Do you ever see yourself giving someone the opportunity to save you?

Sometimes I think about it, but I get scared and although my life might seem tough to some, well it's become easier for me livin' like this than changin' things.

Soundscape

Intro

(Audio - traffic sounds from the A14)

Lost in a rumour (1) - Voice of relative

The drone of the motorway

an all night cafe

in the fade fade fadeaway

she's lost in a rumour

(Audio - garage forecourt / distant drag of boy racers)

Eternal - Voice of narrator

It's been four months since I've seen you

your hair somewhat longer

and you've become something of a fashion icon

even in your unlaced trainers you remain elegant

your frame just fits into these surroundings

when you move you glide

and when you speak you never waste a single word

an economy of language, perhaps evolving

from so many police interviews,

but there again, I think it's how you really are

I wrote 'Lover' for you

and tonight you read it for the first time

you smile, and hold it close

and will put it on the wall

of your latest short term accommodation

wherever that might be

in the territory that you inhabit

in the glow of neons and pylons

and never ending diversion signs

(Working girl - whispers)

Dirt faced angel dropped your wand,
battle hardened bottle blonde

(Audio - cash machine / petrol pumps)

Tesco Metro - Voice of narrator

Standing there
majestic again
soft pencil lines
on a Tesco Metro skyline
dressed as an alibi
in the white plague plastic universe
tonight, let's rewrite the copy
and tell it like it really is
out there....yeah?
destination nowhere
pay and display
display and you'll pay
jettison - cancel the cheque
love bites on your neck
and what you see is what you'll get
out there
in the galaxy of chevrons and pylons
and passwords and user names
forget it babe
I'm driving through walls of silence
lay on your back for another 20 minutes
and gaze at stars you'll never see
you'll forget me
easily

(Audio - amusement arcade)

Lost in a rumour (2) - Voice of witness

Lone figure on a coastline
a flicker on the skyline
a murmur on a phone line
she's lost in a rumour

(Audio - railway track / bridges)

Night Train - Voice of narrator

Trespass, staring into blackness
transfixed on a quasi horizon
azure eyed princess
alone on the night train
expressionless
in a pawn shop window
your price faded by the sunlight
perpetrator
slashed face in a doorway
in the fade fade fadeaway
fingers
feverishly running
eating from a tin can
wavering and cunning
on a sunbed in Nacton
a few hours from action
inhaling
sweet intoxication
in The Angel Hotel
occasional shot
flicking through the classifieds

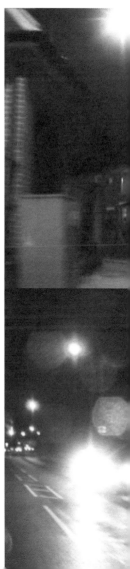

a time bomb ticking
when you testified to this
your life story
on a cigarette packet
a rabbits foot in a stolen jacket
and you never knew it was there
could it make any difference
from this living disorder
black box recorder

(Additional voiceover - whispers)

Reflections of a silver blade in the neon fade

(Audio - high heels in subway at night)

Lost in a rumour (3) - Voice of hoodie

There's a rustle in the hedgerow
a tremor in the contra flow
a shiny red stiletto
she's lost in a rumour

(Audio - youths at night)

She said - Voice of narrator

So here we stand in the black sky neon circus
treading needles in the acupuncture wasteland
on the tropic of torture with your alter ego
with the script for your third phone-in to vibe city radio
from nerve gas alley of users and abusers
behind the kebab house and lesbian bar
coerced and co-framed and you lean against the fence

with your nail file and hard house
where you break into cars sleep naked on the backseat
and I distinctly remember you saying these words
'men are killing women'
as you looked straight ahead gazed out through the windscreen
into a future that held nothing but panic

(Additional voiceover - whispers)

Left your scent and marked the cards, staked your claim in
ev'ry yard

(Audio - taxi office)

Hustlers and Infidels - Voice of narrator

If I could catch your shadow
for a brief moment
on the wall outside the taxi office in Neale Street
well, that would be something
but I'm always 10 minutes behind your moves
and that 10 minutes can amount to a lifetime
time spent with you is time spent without you
and even though I'm learning fast
I'm never fast enough
I've got your words from the latest broadcast
a three way link up with your dealers
that I play back in this cul-de-sac
of flight simulation heroin and crack
and thank you
you've given me another scene another cameo
that I had to experience to appreciate
it's value added input to the script
that is growing bit by bit

your footsteps, I didn't get to hear them
but I imagine them disappearing up the hill
past the floodlit church around the corner
and into a waiting car with another £40 worth of substance
in your bloodstream shot up in the backroom
and payed for in advance by our backers
who are even further off the case than I
but I'm getting closer
and the prospect of being there for the take
excites me more than ever

(Audio - police car sirens)

1.57am

(Different narrator for each verse)

The night grows ever dim
you're in the skin you're in
double dealing in sin
not a glimmer within

then you see a distant face
and quicken the pace
into a cul-de-sac
you come under attack

and you turn away and run
burning rubber from the scum
and you're slumped against the wall
deleting the call

your make up it's all run
the night is all undone

the contents of your bag
lay scattered all around
the fragments of your life
shattered, run aground

and you light a cigarette
shaking put it to your lips
and you're aching for a hit
and you're breaking up a bit

(Audio - part transcript from social service
report)

Poison - Voice of Katie

She called me mummy
they called me druggie
they stole her from me
my world went empty
I am poison, I am scum
I am not worthy of anyone

I run with the foxes
I walk with the vagrants
I watch the snowflakes
make patterns on the pavement
I am poison, I am scum
I am not worthy of anyone

Don't ask me round
don't know this frown
I'm a single noun
I'm out of town

I am poison, I am scum
I am not worthy of anyone

And if you dare to let me in
I'll promise you one thing
I will destroy everything
I'll be your ruin, your undoing
I'll take your stuff
sell it for drugs
I am the unloved
I can't be touched

They cut out my heart
took me apart
they froze my mind
they made me blind

I came from the womb
I'm headed for my tomb
someone cry for me
at my funeral please

Am I poison?, am I scum?
cry for me, someone

(Audio - tower block)

Lost in a rumour (4) - Voice of dealer

Bad dreams in the high rise
there's a scream from the low rise
undercover of night skies
she's lost in a rumour

(Audio / ambient sounds from industrial estate)

In your skin - Voice of narrator

It's all here on your skin and in your skin
on your clothes and in your hair
you bring it on and you bring it in
I pull you close can breathe your lifestyle
it tells me where you've been and what you've been doing
for the last 12 hours
nicotine gasolene and a dream that blew out long ago
Dove perfume and a seedy room
fast food and your semi nude sleep walk
when you rip down curtains
and smash into wardrobe doors with your fists clenched
throwing bathroom mirrors out of hotel windows at dawn
your storm, will it ever relent?
you're here again, you always come back
and though your actions scare me
I have grown to need the drama that you bring
this thing has drawn me in somehow

(Additional voiceover - whispers)

Every hour a different lover, on a postcard undercover

(Audio - cafe sounds / coffee machines etc
and a bus terminal)

Blue Money - Voice of narrator

The bus station cafe
this is the ideal setting for your seminar
'A masterclass in resilience'

that classic shot of spoon in cup stirring and stirring
you know how it goes
and there's a frame that we re-visit
the red streak in your black hair
the cracked teeth and the cold stare
and last night in your red skirt and red tights
prowling through the dirt by the warehouse lights
where you shoot on sight and you shoot to kill
and you fall and you rise 'cause you've got the will
to overcome it all somehow
this is a masterclass in resilience
blue sky thinking?
that is never an issue
not here
living off blood in fun town where you run run run around
you're overground and you're underground
lost but never found
not any more
because I can see now the destiny and the glory
of no fixed abode
an open road that runs somewhere and nowhere together
and that state of being that I can see in your eyes
and you're lifted above it in the Suffolk skies
and look down on it to try and make some sense
but, why does anything have to make sense?
and you're still stirring your coffee
when we see them coming towards us
and you smile
and I never quite understood why you smiled
but why does anything have to make sense?

Lost in a rumour (5) - Voice from police car radio

Sirens echo by the roadside
shadows crawl across the kerbside
petrol burning on a kids slide
she's lost in a rumour

(Audio / telephone conversation from a call box)

Revelations - Voice of narrator

And I'm thinking of you
sitting in The Blue Moon Cafe around 11.30am
with your fingers locked around your coffee mug
to keep them warm
making patterns on the table cloth
your large grey eyes
against what I once described
as 'the incredible trademark surround'
your Mancunian accent, 200 miles from home
what is home?
'Longest time I've spent in one place in the last eight years
is six months, and that was in prison,
but that is the way I live'
despite all this, your living space
which I estimated to be no more than 120 square feet
had some kind of brilliance about it
in my eyes anyway
the fact that you could re-invent it so frequently
by taking virtually nothing with you each time you left
was one of the most impressive things I have ever witnessed
and strange, when you opened the ripped curtains
there was always a film going on outside

Lost in a rumour (6) - Voice of working girl

A mirage in the moonlight
vignette in the twilight
fade fading from sight
she's lost in a rumour

(Audio - Orwell Bridge and Europark)

Search Party - Voice of narrator

And I will fire coloured flares
up into the night skies from the Orwell Bridge
that light up the Euro park
a one man search party with your picture around my neck
laminated for protection from the elements
even though this may all be in vain
some fait accompli
I will trawl the taxi ranks, kebab houses,
drop-in centres and 24 hour pharmacy
sit on the bowling alley steps out in the rain
tigers eyes on a mission in the mist
lighting beacons, building fires in the multi-storeys
shout your name through tannoys in the disused railway tunnel
where I once saw you injecting at 4 in the morning
I will comb the back alleys and empty factories till daylight
the cafes, laundrettes and subways
in my pocket the things that you gave me
a PJ Harvey cd, a poem that you wrote for me in a crayon
that you found outside your daughter's school
where you watched her from the fence
and she may never know who you are

(Audio - traffic / medics etc)

Lost in a rumour (7) - Voice of taxi driver

In a rear view mirror
an airbrushed picture
in late October
she's lost in a rumour

(Audio - police car radio)

Glance - Voice of narrator

A glance
paid back with interest
quickfire the tempest
beckons in the wings
an angel sings in the Esso neon drag
unnerving but instinctive
hanging in the sidestreets
the fever and the fury
it lives on forever
Number 79
all boarded up now
I can't hear you breathing anymore
I don't see your eyes changing colours
but your whispers
how they haunt me
sirens scream in the distance
futile resistance
tonight I saw it all...
what I gave you the night you called
hot water for your instant coffee
some indigestion tablets

that I wrapped in a tissue
and put in your jacket pocket
I watched the CCTV
held it on freeze frame for 3 days
ate out of tin cans
just like you taught me
slept on the reclaimed sofa
remembering what you said

(Voice of Katie)

'Who needs houses?'
'Who needs anything?'
'You take the journey to a place beyond it'
'safe in this skin, don't need anything -
'cause the drugs, they fucking work man
blocks it all out, like really blocks it all out,
like the best fucking therapy you could ever got'

(Voice of narrator)

I will sit in a cafe
in a seaside resort, out of season
and wait for someone like you
to walk by and glance inside

(Audio - can blowing in the wind)

Lost in a rumour (8) - Voice of newscaster

Fallen from a bridge
flotsam on the drift
blow blowing a kiss
she's lost in a rumour

(Audio - hospital sounds - heart monitor etc)

Talisman - Voice of narrator

Yes, it is I your talisman who appears before you
at the end of this hospital bed as you slip in and out...
I'm holding a lighter above my head
swaying softly from side to side in adoration
I've been here all night listening to your dreams
that I know to be more than dreams
the labyrinth of hallwalls where you gouged messages
on doorways with your nail file
and the screwdriver you found in the back of a taxi
before you went missing for 12 desperate hours
ripping out flowers on the sea front
they cut your pretty face after the curfew
and I tasted the blood and the tears on you
as we walked back to the hotel in the rain
where you worked as a waitress for £5 an hour
and the occasional tip
kissed your lips on the boardwalk in a dream
in an amusement arcade in another
the lover found scaling a wall
caught up in barbed wire
heart of fire
the DC walking round and round your head pounding
as I waited outside most of the night
yes, it is I
your talisman
who will never leave your side

(All audio references are to give a rough guide)

Poetics

The Open

You seem shy...almost apologetic
as you inspect this latest concept
in living and work space
in this former store room in an industrial unit
up here where the air is clear and our minds are clear
I pull you near
you come gift wrapped in mystery
weaving your tapestry of intrigue through these shadows
and the words that you say
they may just stay with me
'the moon looks bright tonight'
'would you like a jelly baby?'
things that may seem insignificant at the time
can become a catalyst for something far bigger
than either of us could possibly imagine
your hair is tied back and I ask you to let it down
I put on 'Lovers in the rain' by The Open
pulled you in, whispering, nothing much
something about your eyes I think
who knows
this could lead to the longing
the wanting
the yearning
the tossing and turning night after night
the craving
aching hearts breaking into splinters
through longest winters

Tomorrow Night

Since our 'blind date' last Friday night
I've been thinking about you from time to time...
well, actually no, that's not strictly true
because I have been thinking about you pretty much constantly
for days now...the nights too
wanting to call you, but holding back
waiting for the right time, just in case
in case you said no
or worse still...nothing
blanked the call maybe
people do that don't they?
an easy way out
I thought about calling you Monday, too early?
prssre - is that what West End girls txt to friends
not that you're a West End girl, far from it
Sunderland - home to The Golden Virgins no less
I mentioned it last week when you were here
but it bounced off you
Tuesday came, then Wednesday
I resisted until a few moments ago
your phone rang 4 times
then you answered, you said little - perhaps you are shy
but you said 'yes, that would be nice'
and as you don't drive
we could meet at the same place at eight
and I feel, like the feeling you get
at the beginning of something
that may just be...the beginning of something
a warm tingle...and I wonder,
I wonder all kinds of things

Wolf

This three quarter length coat
fits you so perfectly
bespoke and made to measure
clings to your '82 Wearside frame
cutting shapes in the out-take break light superdome
our habitual home in the a.m. portal
'like your coat'
'It's not mine, I borrowed it from my room mate'
we meet at the border crossing
where the headlights rotate and create illusions
'risking it all'
but without the danger there would be no drama
and without drama we are not living
there is only so long we can stay on the seabed
our habits and our hunger rushing to the surface
to devour then return
you to your tinned food and daytime tv
me, to this incense fragranced universe
we could take things further
maybe move things forward a little
do what normal people do
what do they do?
restaurants and cinemas perhaps
dinner parties
coffee and carrier bags in Bluewater on Saturdays
it seems a world away from this
and fuck it
does it really have any appeal anymore?

Talking to you

Begged, borrowed and stolen...
I can see that now
it's not just something that people say
not in your case anyway
I asked you where you spent Christmas Day
'Peterborough Prison'
so you got done for shop lifting clothes
in a win win situation
you either got to keep the clothes or got caught
and did three weeks
you got caught - your preferred option
with your own private room in a quiet corridor
with a brand new television
'not much difference from a hotel really,
the main difference being that it is free
and all the meals are provided'
I can see that you've come so far
and that there is no stigma involved
and this is what I learn during our conversations
allowing you to smoke your rollies
blowing smoke rings
in my strictly non smoking environment
and you look me in the eye
and everything about you is truth despite its origins
could we create anything from this?
something outside this project?
strange how things have progressed
all the taped interviews
trying to explain things to the police
I keep the things they gave me
little white plastic tubes and pieces of paper
dealing with all their questioning
their psyche, their prying

and tonight it's the blue lights again
but they just don't seem to get it do they?
we explain, they stand there with glazed expressions
it's all in reverse, them, us, this
turning itself upside down
the one with the clearest head by a mile is you
because you know what fear is
facing it all and dealing with everything
that is thrown at you with consummate ease
everything has become so mad
that it is even becoming normal to me
we've got the Big Story
a year of this now and I can't begin to remember it all
even with an 80,000 word journal to help me
3 books of poetry and a filmscript all but finished
it moved so fast, and we have come full circle
several times over
and I still have the killer stuff to write
about the body parts in the freezer
I've been saving that for the ending
when maybe there will be no ending
just a new beginning

SPARKFILMS

Half Light

I have good reason to be here
that is what I tell myself
with you, in the back of a car in this delivery yard
on an industrial estate in the half light at 1.47am
sparks flying from your fingertips
some deft movement of your hips
you cried once into a tissue
I held you, and after all that you had been through
it was a rare moment of emotion for which you apologised
you had no need to...
we're all going through something
I should know
I'm even being polite to the guys
trying to sell me mobile telephones from call centres
on the sub continent
the only people I converse with in the daylight hours
since I shut myself away from her
from it
from everything
even though they get my name wrong and are very persistent
I try my best through the delays the crackle and distortion
and yeah, I feel I wanna be nice to someone
and it should be you
because one day things may be different for both of us
in the half light
in this twilight land we make our own
holding hands
but so alone

Antispace

Intelligent landing?
into the night zone, this grainy texture, potent mixture
you will be hiding, hiding in the antispace
climbing above me, the security light, it catches your face
we could talk about violent crime on the streets
or we could get lost in the moment
you have voted with your eyes, I can see them now
but only just
a week may pass and a glance into the kitchen
may reveal the shampoo and eyeliner you rip from magazines
between your telephone rage and adjusting the fairy lights
extremes that can no doubt be traced back
to your childhood

SPARKFILMS

Lover

Two and a half sugars in your tea
the way you look at me when I'm looking at you
shyness is a virtue
you left your KitKat wrapper in the kitchen
where you deal in one word answers
except when explaining about the Kosovan who beat you up
and you sit in my car, your hair it falls on your shoulders
you say nothing and do nothing but in these moments
you mean everything
sometimes sitting on my sofa looking at your phone
I notice the art of your ankles in high heels
against the grey of the fabric
because I see you in detail and I love what I see
and what I do not hear
kissed your eyes and asked a question
that would have a one word answer
has anyone else ever kissed your eyes?
I thought not, your eyes, childlike sometimes
and the white is whiter
than the bright lights of the motorway...

Skate on by

Euphoric sky, eye to eye, skate on by
an Avenue Taxis customer receipt
eleven black biro numerals heavenly terminals
there's a radiance in the glow of the containers
there's a silence in the stillness
broken by heels on the concrete steps
the key turning in the door to your flat above the pizza joint
that acts as a nerve centre from eleven till dawn
where demons are born trailed round in the tail lights
until mid summer night's dream may just evaporate in the haze
erased by this therapy, this solace
and through the window some mystic faith healer
is reaching down from the clouds dancing in the rhythmic flow
with the promise of some harmonic ending and rebirth
eye to eye, skate on by

SPARKFILMS

Interzone

Bare light bulb, spirit of youth
this naked truth that lays on the floor in the crossfire
friend and enemy this is the interzone of destiny
you put on your high heels, doing deals turning wheels
your mind is numb and your body is numb
you bite the bullet never turn and run
'cause the bullet can't harm you
safe in your skin, wild angel with wings
always running through the back doors of your mind
feeding on poison, bleeding in a prison cell
seizing the moment, intricate timing
takeaways and breakaways you'll be blazing at dawn
a thorn in my soul

SPARKFILMS

Missing

We arranged to meet at 11 the next morning
on a bench near the cemetery opposite Oxfam
perfect, this was the kind of territory we had become used to
you showed me the photo identikit picture
they had made of you
'It's nothing like me, is it'
and I had to agree
'do you know why?...'cause it aint me - it's Della
they caught her on the cameras and put two and two together
and ended up with about sixty fucking eight
anyways I'm keepin' out their way while this is going down'
we go to your secret underground bunker
where you've spent the last 10 days
just 50 meters from the high street
only you could discover a place like this
a door with no number, no letter box
nothing other than a splash of graffiti
and a chubb lock that you somehow have a key for
a concrete staircase down to room with no windows
with a semi open plan toilet
with cracked wash basin to match
no hot water, no lecci
but I knew that I would just love it here
heating and lighting by way of 200 stolen candles
a mattress pulled from a skip at 3am
assorted duvets and blankets from a 'friend'
and you're writing poetry again across the walls
'star gazer trail blazer amaze me dazzle me and daze me'
we will dance in the cemetery at dawn

Rust

You're in this deep
even deeper than before
if that was ever possible
keeper of the stash, a carrier bag of cash
that you use as a pillow, an expensive one at £16,000
the booty keeper, night creeper, light sleeper
down here in the gravel, the dust and the rust
the walls are seeping
and you're not sleeping like you used to
and I'm watching you imagining the pictures that you see
and the voices that you hear
as you spiral downwards
falling from an airplane
breaking into pieces
hanging from a cliff face
drowning in a whirlpool
you shake, and waking your eyes open
but you don't see me
just an interrogators dazzle
some fatalistic tailspin
a feather in a headwind
crying in a hedgerow
dying on death row, then suddenly you leap
your nails claw down the wall
you're not dreaming anymore
this is far worse

The Silent City

Checking your eye shadow on the elevator to the 9th floor
where you overhear a conversation about a psychic
who may know the identity of a serial killer
who wrapped his victims in 10 metres of gauze
with holes cut out to show the eyes
their mouths drawn with lipstick, smiling
natron on a shelf in a room with a two way mirror
and the wired exterior
and here now
through a triple glazed window gazing at the traffic flow
in the silent city where all the taxis
are running out of control
in a state of unrest, your heart beating faster
as you approach Room 226

Final Eliminator

Sex girl in a crack world on the rat talk catwalk
attacks drag queen in the full beam
where are you now? what are you now?
self sealed in foil,
cut open and reveal all this sunny morning
some tabloid android gargoyle spewing in the gutter
where all the glitter hearts and body parts
get soaked up in the void
retouched and ripped open, this is the final eliminator
a futuristic sculpture, skeletal wires
dormant in a field of static, no touch transmission
no one can save you now

I saw all of this

We walked up the concrete steps
to your flat above the estate agents
I remember how you dropped your key
and your words as I picked it up
'I'm not drunk, well actually perhaps I am, just a little'
the babysitter was asleep on the sofa
and I will always remember
how you touched her hair and whispered 'night night Hayley'
as you pulled the duvet over her shoulder
it told me so much about you
we sat in the kitchen
you put on the television and lit up a rollie
sitting there with the window open in the still of night
watching the twinkling lights of the container ships
a headline from a magazine caught my eye
something about crystal meth
there was vodka on your breath
and the space between us was closing
at 4am I heard the pitter patter of tiny feet
and the softest and most beautiful voice that said 'mummy'
some angelic vision in a white nightdress
how she stood beside you and placed her doll on your pillow
I saw all of this

Reactor

Flash of eyelash
pulled up your coat collar and your hair was blowing back
reactor
street corner supanova
time was when I became obsessive about someone like you
coming through into the sanctuary of this inner space
rapacious thriller killer in lace
and I'm facing it all head on
hint
skin sin
heady scene in the edited dream of 'the curse of the kiss'
come a little closer said the jailer
watch the trailer while I slowly undress you
you won't notice a thing
stay fanatical
there's a picture in the supplement
all glossy sultry and seductive
it could easily be you
what do you think?
blink
you're a death wish waiting in the shadows
tongue
'the movable muscular structure in the mouth -
it is used for tasting'
and speaking?
ravenous in the hallway

Step back into it

Your glittering career
it started here
across this table all those months ago
your eyes were much brighter then
and I've kept the Golden Virginia hand rolling tobacco paper
that you left on the sofa all this time
I wonder why?
some keepsake before I let you loose
with your performing arts degree, to step back into it
with all the mainliners
tonight, asking you all this, in our Q&A session
relayed straight into an FM radio station
'tell me how they get the stuff into prisons'
'explain how all this has affected your menstrual cycle'
'are you personally aware of the numbness'
the radio station are paying £400 for this
and like our initial deal back in March
you will get 50%
before you step back into it
only this time you're gonna have to keep on walking
'cause I've taken this thing as far as I can now
and do I blame myself for your rapid demise?
I suppose the answer is 'yes'
even though you answered the small ad

Hunger

Tentatively you step into the room
my eyes they follow you
not the kind of decor you might expect to see
your movement circumspect at first
slightly ill at ease
then, melting just a little
when you read what I wrote for your friend
'some guardian angel appearing out of the mist
in your darkest moment...a luminescent being
with the third eye masterplan...'
you seem reassured
that six months after her death
I was trying in my own way, however futile that may have been
to save her
I show you the note
that she posted through the door last November
'Really sorry I missed you - need your help
please call me soon as, Katie x'
you cry
I hold you
'this must have been written just days before she died'
then you show me the two of you together smiling
in a supermarket photobooth

Yarmouth Road

Under the Wilco sign
on the Yarmouth Road in the orange glow
in the toxic haze, floating
grazed and bruised, blazed abused in shapes and shadows
this inter dimensional glowing orb
two hours old in towels and bubble wrap
eyes wide open on a ninth floor stairwell by a liftshaft
this concrete ghetto, echo chamber of faceless strangers
a message on a cardboard box
'mummy loves you, see you on the other side'
saw you
in a hand tinted photograph laughing
in The Fox and Hounds
in angels wings and glitter things drinking Breezers
you walked over the bridge one more time
crossed the line
when I heard your voice one last time
'and tear the stained skin from my harlot brow'
and I'm lost between the real and the make believe
an illusion and the infrared
the camera never lies?
the damp bank notes tainted with lavender
still in the carrier bag at the roadside

Auto Erotic Asphyxiation

You need credit
your hair is still wet
as I watch you walking into the bright lights
you must have taken me into your trust
as you leave your 'paper work' on the seat beside me
'read it if you want'
which I do - tick boxes as well?
fucking hell, I feel privileged
that I already knew your 'true identity'
I listen to the radio, a phone in
on auto erotic asphyxiation
until a caller from Middlesbrough draws their last breath
you run back in your boots and your jeans
and your black top
you left your coat in the car
and that always makes me think that you will return
though it is no guarantee
several roundabouts and about a dozen turnings later
we arrive
you are true to your word
'turn off the fucking lights...I don't want them to see
which car I came in'
you stand by a phone box like you said
then I see him in a white hooded top
you disappear for a moment then return and show me the stuff
it's 3am and we watch them
the milkman, the railway maintenance guys
the footballer, was it him?
the nurse
we eat chocolate and crisps and you say
'you really write about this?
yeah...

Aeroplane Seats

I'd not heard from you in a while
then...'hey, it's me...'
you could appear anywhere at any time
on television once at a Greenpeace demonstration
just knew it was you, the kick boxing gave it away
your 8 stone 5 pound a la mode frame
that has graced many a festival dance tent
then one night on the radio
when I was driving back from London at midnight
news of a group of people laying in front of a missile carrier
at an airbase in Somerset
blocking its way onto the A361
I knew you would never miss out on an opportunity like that
but the real killer that I was to hear about 3 months later
as we sat on some aeroplane seats
you and your friends took from a 747 during a refuel
was how the guys blew up a 6 million pound fighter plane
just 100 yards from security
we spent 3 nights at your sister's semi in Lowestoft
ate pizzas and listened to 'Cavelleria Rustincana'
you took barbiturates, they seemed to make little impression
and we got a call to say we were being watched by MI5
you, so dismissive saying 'who gives a fuck'
and I dread the day when I walk into the room
and you're standing there smoking in the way that you do
listening to 'The thrill is gone' by BB King

Christmas

17 minutes until your driver arrives
it's cold outside and I'm glad we can talk about lifestyle
from your standpoint anyway
in a Sainsbury's car park at 1.43am
I gather information, you interest me
there is daytime and there is night
but not for you
you go to sleep around 6am and wake some 12 hours later
and by doing so put yourself
in some kind of alternative universe
which you deem to be normal
and I can see your point of view
you are never demanding,
in fact I feel some kind of inner peace
when we are together like this
gradually over the months we have developed
some kind of understanding
an opening up, even trust
you teach me about myself and how our lives
run in some kind of parallel
and I wish
I wish you would come and stay for Christmas
even though you might spend most of it sleeping
and I would stand over you and make three wishes
that you are loved
have children
and are truly happy one day...

Crossfire

So you're still out there
between the van hire and The Blue Moon Cafe
in the crossfire with your afterburners and the akimbo stance
stepping into traffic in an aerosol vapour trail
blowing out sensors crossing enemy lines
we go back to your place with the boarded up front door
and the back door has been kicked in
but I like your innovative use of the velvet curtains
you pulled from a skip
along with selected items of furniture
in this stylish home makeover done on a low budget
in fact, done on nothing at all
you were always a born survivor
you introduce me to your 'friends'
a transvestite
a vampire
and a murderer
a murderer?
he seems by far the most rational to me
with an in-depth knowledge of Darwinian theory
and he did have the decency to give his wife
5 private burials at her favourite locations
and rather touching
what he wrote in her blood on the bathroom wall
'My darling Lilian, you are free now'
and this commune that you live in
'a small group of people living communally
and sharing in work earnings etc'
maybe a place that I could settle for a while
after my 'time' away, I call it a sabbatical
to those few people who recognise me now
and ask where I have been for the past few years

Flash of Light

In the sunburn afterburn alleyway they hunt in packs
you pose, splashed with colour run for cover
by the wheelie bins and wheel trims
a flash of light picture postcard framed
and it feels like diamonds sometimes
teeth marks on your skin and it's a straight choice
between the vice squad and the firing squad
the blood splattered backdrop
all this on the same day three more products were reclaimed
from supermarket shelves and a chinese shopowner
was found dead laying over a safe in Wigan
and in your head did you ever think about breaking away?
I always wondered that
a sweet wrapper twisting and tumbling
from a ninth floor balcony
where the television had been on for 48 hours
plays tricks with your eyes
open a book, see a picture of a table laid for one
light the touch paper and run

SPARKFILMS

Billboards and Daytime TV

So you're scaling this urban metropolis
its sunken eyes and cries of plastic dolls
on conveyerbelts in the speed dial hitman daylight
and we're standing shoulder to shoulder
by another telephone mast cemented into the ground
only yesterday, outcasts in this brave new world
of sex slaves and cheap flights from the Ukraine
tube shootings, lootings, watered down pop in DIY superstores
where Simon got a job and saved himself
from almost certain death
though he still goes back to his bedsit
above the garage and puts on eye liner in a £6.99 mirror
and thinks of his mother
who died in a fire ten years ago tonight

SPARKFILMS

Subway Fire

I've been sitting on the landing for over an hour now, waiting
just like you said, looking at weeks of junk mail
and all the unopened letters to tenants, one of whom died
in this very hallway three weeks ago
I can sense that you are close now with your night's shopping
in a matchbox walking through some meteor shower
reading a message under the bridge 'Beware Alligator Teeth'
the soles of your shoes still burning from the subway fire
a celluloid fragment on your wrist from Bollywood 95
maybe reading from your book the same lines
'as he pushed her against the wall they were
gorging with desire'
and I have been reading from your book
which hovers above the textural plains at 4am
'and if you shine your brilliant light in these eyes
they will never see another sunrise'
because one day baby, I know you will be gone

Drug Runners

First time I saw you, in combat gear at 1.30am
some kind of overnight bag slung over your shoulder
me, no more than an impartial observer
waiting in the wings for her to arrive
with more of those little things we drop off in the night
for dirty cash
there must be something intoxicating in calcium and water
you, no one's daughter and never were
with an acetylene torch burning off another door
I've long fallen from grace, but there's no turning back
from this fucking crazy lifestyle that got me hooked
and I blame it entirely on no one
things had been far worse before this
receiving 4 death threats in less than a week
all from one source, myself
one minute with you is all it took
on this brilliant road to self mutilation of the mind
the end of mankind in the industrial sprawl
of pallets and enamel and wire
hearts of fire

SPARKFILMS

Film Scripts and Hits

We never planned this, no one could have
the first weekend we slept in a portacabin
that acted as a cafe by day for construction workers
after two nights we moved homes to the Site Manager's Office
where you exchanged a lap top for a drop off at 4am
you were always streets ahead of me in every way
and less than half my age
each day would bring unprecedented excitement and intrigue
and after all, what had I got to lose?
only my wife, my home, my job, in no particular order
oh, and my street cred
and would I ever have to explain this to anyone?
Helen's mother for instance,
can't imagine where I'd start on that one
but it ran through my mind sometimes
when you would go off for hours at a time
but return with Mega Deals and Happy Meals,
cigarettes and wine
and other stuff
and I would think, this could end up in the newspapers,
the courts, prison, after all,
it occurred to me that we broke the law every single day
but after a while this madness took on a strange normality
and I needed it like you needed heroin
and I wanted you like a mother wants her newborn
warm and close, life was becoming instinctive
and I realised by week 3 that I had reached the point
of no return, which proved to me,
that the previous 12 years did not add up to much
I was learning fast, faster than ever,
you taught me how to break into cars
and blow out alarm systems, but bigger.

even bigger that all of this, I was falling in love with you
and that is when I realised,
whatever the result of our actions,
it just had to be you and me in our very own film
that no one else would see, with scenes like this...
'Nobody's Home' by Avril Lavigne blasting out of a car stereo
at 3am on the motorway on replay for a 100 miles,
your hand in my hand, the connection,
the sight of the credit cards you had acquired
after just 36 hours in the North East
laid out on the bed in The Novotel
ordering all your favourite sandwiches from room service
phoning your step dad at dawn,
and telling him that you were going to report him
to Social Services and Hertfordshire Police
for years of abuse
you showed me a picture, of your 2 year old sister Carly
who was killed by a hit and run driver in Luton
at 4.30 in the afternoon on August 8th 1985
which explained to me in an instant
how this all started and how I wanted it to last

We hadn't slept for almost 3 days and nights
it seemed like we were living on pure adrenalin
we got high from being chased by you guys
even in your unmarked cars
we were able to ID you in our rearviews,
it was the way you sat upright and focused
obvious, we became experts
I lost count of the cars we stole
between Middlesbrough and Ipswich
it must have been 8 or 9,
we loved the Tesco sign out there on our very own horizon

people were so kind leaving their vehicles for us
all neatly parked between the white lines
some of those that we 'broke into', well, there was no need
they had left the doors unlocked, and in one case
the key was in the ignition, very thoughtful
British people can be so kind and when you are driving
someone else's BMW into an electricity sub station
the sparks that fly, they just seem brighter
more pronounced somehow
in this world, only idiots possess such statements
of power and lifestyle, when only we know, we have the power
and lifestyle that they can only dream about
while they are sat at the Odeon munching on popcorn
fucking twats

I think back to the four nights we spent in the basement
where we found the body parts in the freezer
carefully packaged in cling film and bubble wrap
blood red dayglo, masking tape blue,
it had little affect on you,
placing frozen peas and McCains Oven Chips
next to the severed foot, your cold blooded nonchalance,
it impressed me, marking time,
of our highest and lowest points
converging reality with fantasy running hand in hand
through the subway, your empiric gutter stance,
it came in waves for days, I was stoned for the most part
you, dangerously close to the end, writing out a guest list
for your funeral, an impressive compilation
of urban white noise on a cd
with your name on the cover 'Katie - She who dares'
when we left on the Tuesday I was tempted,
looking at the phone box - you grabbed my arm

and pulled me back
at the time I almost resisted, but looking back on it now
I can see you were way ahead of me

Traffic - that's what we are
in this car in all these dead beat places
and you're speakin' in some kind of code
language overload, and I'm finding,
finding it really fucking hard
to keep up, keep up with where we are,
working out how you throw them off the scent
with your simultaneous conversations and arm actions
as you point directions on the windscreen
which are different to anything you are discussing
with these people, who are these people?
pretty face neons, a Hollywood gantry with strobes
that threw us for a moment, although it is hard to imagine
anything like that having the least effect on you,
but it did, 'cause you looked over to me as if to say
'what the fuck was that?'
and the roads that we travel on,
dripping, surreal, seeping gas
breathing in and slinking through the haze
the warehouse ablaze on the horizon, lights up the sky
3am eternal, you remember that?
impressive, I can see you through the steam
you seem thinner, and in the vapour trail I find it amazing
that your eyes are clear as crystal
converging and colliding, submerged in the tide
you just take it in your stride
hustler, body extra, sitting by my side

Curled up on the stained settee
your hair, it's in tangles
talking to no one, it must be a week now
the curse of surrender, tactile and tender
the pill box is empty, your eyes frozen over
pins dig so deep, so deep you don't feel them
try and decipher the words you have written
by light of reflections, the night that bought torture
layed in the shadows, smashed out in the basement
I wanted to help you, no one could help you
stared into space, in a trancelike state
terminal forces, the act of a killer
in the cold chill of winter, avoiding the sunscreen
everything fading all turned to mute
send in the stormtroopers, bring on the blitzkreig
cordon the area, in case any kids see
take a mould, cast her in ice
seize the moment, donate it to science

The Sex Life of Aliens

'That you should focus on something that seemed
so insignificant at the time with such detailed precision,
it says something about you'
'I remember everything'
'Throughout all of that and all of this?'
'Yes'
'I'm impressed'
'I always impressed you'
'Yeah'
kisses soft as rain, reflections of cranes
and the night is deadly still
the sex life of aliens, we were untouchable once
our lives taking turns, too many roundabouts made us dizzy
but we were always destined to take the same eventual path
you look better than ever, if that were ever possible
'I used to pick up the strands of your hair
and keep them in an envelope, I never told you that before,
but I'm telling you now'
'You were always mad about me'
'I wrote Dirty Blonde for you'
'Thank you, I love the phone stuff and the bit
about the night I had toothache'

Body Extra

'I wanted it to be like you said, with you playing you,
the things we spoke about, they could have happened
it all came down to timing
by last October you were off the radar
and I'd heard how fucking mad things had got
even by your standards
so I had to make a decision to get someone else
to play your part, imagine trying to brief
a clean living media student from Hertfordshire
well, you've seen the results, it was pretty amazing
but this whole thing starts and ends with you
no matter what happens in between
all the sub plots, they are still evolving
and I see no end to this
it used to occur to me that your phones
were like little disposable cameras with a life cycle
of just a few weeks, or sometimes hours
one thrown from the Orwell Bridge,
another crash landed on the A14 at 70mph at 2am
and something else, the way you went 'shopping'
from service stations, never more than 4 or 5 items at a time
or when you were stealing clothes
with me waiting on the opposite side of the street
my heart pounding, feeling like a criminal
and I never really worked out
if I was guilty of anything'

Synagogues and Coffee Shops

From the summer of your discontent
the flicker of your eyelids
your last tenner spent on gravel
and you're watching it all through mesh
fizzing on your lips
and licking your way to stardom on txt
pixel projection effects
and the enhanced colour of flesh
followed you through synagogues
and coffee shops in the long afternoons
saw the other showgirls hanging out in the basement cafes
killing lines and killing time
out on the blue horizon waiting for the fog to roll in
getting lost in some misty heaven
missing presumed dead
the childlike way you squeezed the blackcurrant carton
and drew from the straw
in the alleyway where the gaslamps used to stand
played right into your hands
your soft face hardened by the city rain
your flame, the blue ice gaze on the casting couch
that day they said blue blood was dripping from your mouth
can still hear the fridge buzzing on the landing
the whirring of sirens out on the ringroad
stuck pins in you
and detected 2 heartbeats as you murmured in Urdu
your heart 4 months in a pawn shop
the fog coming in from the Humber
and you slumber on a reclaimed mattress
in a boarded up end terrace
shriek, taking it deep
they put you to sleep, watching it all through mesh, defenceless

Zero Second Warning System

By the third line
you'd opened up a new chapter in someone else's life
falling in slow motion from a motorway bridge
a starfish x-rayed against the ultra violets
ricochets in the tyretracks
landing by a rosethorn near the roadside
bleeding your beautiful blood in the gaze of Valentino
a week earlier you stood alone defiant
your eyes so full of fire, so full of anger
'we want trees not tarmac'
a one person protest in a field at 10am
Joan of Arc on horseback in the city
torching every lightbox all the colours melting
crushing all the cartons screaming revolution
I saw the cathedral gleaming in the distance
my heart pounding drowning out the traffic
you were putting on your make up
in the splendent song of morning
lowered my guard and revealed my soul
to window shoppers and post grads
cascading around you, the place that I found you
all those months ago, when we went back to the bedsit
saw your face in the fabric of everything
and now at this table I lay out the banknotes
damp and camomile scented,
distant voices running through me merging together
makes me feel
like I don't know how I feel

Gush in Your Throat

I was feeling
feeling tired of the repeat loop
when I heard the clatter
the clatter of shoes on the steel staircase
with its views of brilliant sky
and somehow, just somehow from above you managed to drop
a red and white can of smart priced baked beans from your bag
which was likely to contain further evidence
of your media student lifestyle
in a Suffolk town with an ever growing crime rate
stepping into a blind alley with fire blackened walls
your profile and perfect facial bone structure
shot stars into the sky
we were rainbow, basking in all the white explosions
the gush in your throat, clinging to the sides
and all the beautiful dreams they turn to screams by night
clinging to the walls, the gush in your throat that crushes me now
sends me shaking to the bathroom at 4am
with its pills and razor blades
then it fades a little

SPARKFILMS

Euro Cops in High Speed Chase

You with your 80 mile an hour hair do
talk, talk baby, I'm listening to you, you know I am
out on the amber walk with the Euro cops and bottle tops
it's exciting there
the cold stare, you know I need it only too well
infiltrate me, save me, make me into someone better
hold my hand in the shadows
and tell me about the life of Bobby Sands
for I am the common man and we are connecting
I will sit across a table in a run down restaurant
by the light of a single candle
looking out at the back of a multi storey car park
in any town or city that we just happen to end up in
no more making excuses, we're cutting loose
facing the truth together
subutex, the crucifixion, you will become addition
and I'm nailed to the wall in a hotel room
the future is bright now that we've torn down the walls

Cheap Russian Cigarettes

Just lately I've taken to going out in the early hours
looking for the girl in a turning,
burning cheap Russian cigarettes
waiting in the austere blitz, all carnal and celluloid
how could a bruise look so fucking amazing on anyone?
and I heard what you said through the drone of the sirens
'I would assassinate anybody for money'
'take me back to the asylum by dawn'
'we can only survive so long in this caldron'
'do you hear blood gushing from black youth?'
at war with my instinct, crushed by your imprint
'cause just lately we've seen the face
of a cold blooded killer
in the mirror in a hallway, you with your bare legs in heels
a vein protruding behind your left knee
spitting, breathing deeper
wipe the sleep from your mouth you renegade dreamer
dream bathed in the black rain till dawn
your phone, it went off through the night

SPARKFILMS

Essence

Found on a post-it note in a phone box
'Emily - circus performer and lion tamer in town now'
a break-in at some portacabin in the early hours
shadow dance and squirm, turn towards the trailer park
burn out the tyre tracks, essorant and bareback
this rodeo show for one night only, essence,
essence of you,
new improved taste, new improved formula
while the fire eaters and snake charmers
and bare knuckle fighters in white hoods
load white label goods
into waiting vans as the town sleeps
to the anthem of onward christian soldiers
marching into the void
ever deeper, I am your keeper for the next few hours
your aerosol calling card by arclight in the goods yard
on the multi-wheeled transporters
where Nordic drivers sex dream 'Emily performed here'

Eyes of a Killer

I think back to last morning in the Blue Moon cafe
the two of you sitting at the table under the staircase
together in conversation, you were looking into his eyes
then looking away with that degree of fortitude
that you possess, that in the circumstances was admirable
turning your head in the way that you do,
slowly to the left, then to the right,
as you scan those around you
you played the part with understated brilliance
incredible to think that most of those who sat around you
were working undercover,
we envy your natural state of detachment
and quite understand how you innocently befriended
a cold blooded killer

SPARKFILMS

Filmscape

Dirty Blonde at the Cash Machine - The Film

Sometime around March 2006 I began collating the writing and research I was collecting into the Ipswich underworld. By this time I had over 70 poetic pieces, some general notes about the background, and perhaps most importantly, a series of transcripted interviews with sex workers.

It was a scene that offered a view into an alternative world, and I felt that there was some kind of story to be told on a number of various levels.

My objective was to illustrate different aspects of this world that would give a deeper insight into the people that operate within it, the plots and subplots, all of them interwoven into a complex tapestry of broken dreams.

Although this was a world that interested me there would be no guarantee that it would interest enough members of the general public to create an audience that would make it into something that was commercially viable to produce.

At its base, the concept that was developing into a filmscript had two central characters at its core - a sex worker, and a client - commonly known as a punter.

It occurred to me that two life stories could be told alongside one another and that differing emotional experiences and values could be portrayed.

What I was really doing was re-inventing myself as another character from a different background to tell one side of the story, or at least, a similar emotional and traumatic journey.

The other character was something I was able to create by doing a kind of cut and paste of two working girls.

What follows is the outline story and background information that was sent out to film production companies to see if anyone would be interested in an attempt to get funding and turn this into a feature film.

I have left the outline exactly as it was presented in its raw state. At this stage it did not include a subplot that featured an Eastern European gang who were taking girls off the streets of Ipswich and holding them in a compound.

(Outline follows)...

Concept / Overview / History

My personal situation (the break down of a relationship) had necessitated the need to try and escape from where I found myself emotionally - in a deep and dark pit. Utterly crushed and broken. Although I realised it might not be possible, it was a deliberate decision to enter what I described as a 'twilight underworld' which might take me on a journey through experience that would act as a form of escapism.

Experiences in this - part real / part fantasy environment were documented in a book of word / image (poetry) that was released on March 1st 2006. The title 'piece' - 'Dirty Blonde at the Cash Machine' was based on events that occurred one Saturday between midnight and about 5.30 in the morning.

About half of the content in the book was 'inspired' / influenced by a girl known as 'Katie' who was funding her drug addiction by working as a prostitute in the Red Light District of Ipswich.

We had a series of liaisons which I found of great interest. Her behaviour and on the spot decision making fascinated me. The difference in how someone in her predicament operates on a day to day basis began to write its own story (inside another that I was documenting). Some of this activity appears in a poetic form in 'Dirty Blonde at the Cash Machine'.

After a few months we lost contact. Time passed. I concentrated on book production and so on. Then some 9 months later a similar situation emerged with another girl whose life was even more extreme - and held even more fascination.

I began to write more material for another poetry based book, only this time the stuff that was happening had such an edge to it that it actually felt like we were appearing in a real life film drama.

Although I was happy with the content in 'Dirty Blonde' I felt strongly that the new material had a definite link running through it and might have more potential.

During some of these liaisons I was almost hallucinating with the power of the imagery that either happened for real or was being extended and improvised in my imagination. I documented this as a series of thought patterns and returned to it hours later to turn it into a form of poetry.

The escapism from the deep personal trauma that I had been searching for 9 months beforehand was suddenly magnified to such an extent that I found myself living in a world that was both true and make believe. The power of reality merging with the journey of my imagination.

The experiences led to a period of time where I converted them through my writing into both poetry and a journal that I was keeping that was gradually evolving as part of a possible film.

During this time I was developing a 'third person scenario' that might act as a vehicle to tie the thing together somehow.

I visualised the person in my position as being in a marriage (mine was not a marriage) with a family / profession / lifestyle etc and how devastating this situation could be and to look at the thing from this perspective. This also allowed some of the freedom of documentary style analysis. I projected the experience of the male having a breakdown during this time which also opened up the lack of logic in his subsequent decision making.

I was moving towards a 'relationship' between two people whose lives were completely off the rails - but for entirely different reasons and how they could go on an adventure that was reckless / exciting / and free.

Their journey would evolve into its own form of escapism verging on fantasy. The backdrop to all of this is one of takeaways / fast food joints / b&b's / motels / sleeping in stolen cars - portacabins - car chases with drug gangs / police and so on. Much of this happened for real while I was researching the material.

There are run down resorts / small towns / 'A' roads / garage forecourts / all very English. Shop lifting / court appearances etc. There are conversations in some of the quieter moments that reveal much of the truth that lays beneath the surface. The girl has had a terrible childhood. Bit by bit her story emerges.

A kind of love story unfolds. Questions are asked about perceived values in lifestyle. During this time the audience may be made to question themselves on how we can all become conditioned to going through the ordinary / the everyday / the nothingness....which amounts to the sad reality of a repeat loop.

The Story

Stephen McKenna has been keeping a secret from his friends and from himself. His marriage is in crisis. Despite a glittering career and comfortable lifestyle Stephen is 'all consumed' by Deborah his wife who he met at university while they were studying law 15 years ago.

She has stopped loving him. He loves her stronger than ever. There is no way back to what they had shared, but he pushes it to the back of his mind hoping that things will go back to how they were.

He is out with a friend one night who tells him that Deborah has been having an affair for 6 months. Stephen is crestfallen and in deep shock.

He goes back to the house and confronts her. He breaks down. The children wake and see their dad on the stairs crying and shaking.

Stephen moves into his friend's spare room. He is suffering from depression. His work suffers. He thinks about Deborah constantly. After a few days it becomes evident to his work colleagues that he needs to take some 'time out'.

But things get even worse.

One night Stephen finds himself in the Red Light District of his local town. He has a disastrous liaison with a girl in his car which makes things even worse than they already were, but as he is driving away he catches a quick glimpse of Katie who will change his life.

She is standing by the Audi dealership and Stephen feels her eyes penetrate his inner soul. For the first time in years he is attracted to someone other than Deborah, and despite the origin of the 'meeting' he becomes strangely captivated by her.

He returns to the same spot several times, he catches a glimpse of her getting into a car one night.

Then one night he sees her. His heart pounding. She gets in his car and they have a fifteen minute encounter. He gets her mobile number.

After he sees her a couple more time he begins to believe that he is having some form of relationship with her. Katie starts calling him to ask favours. She needs to be taken to dealers at all hours of the night.

Katie fascinates Stephen. He begins to see her as a 'therapy' from his situation. She presents an opportunity for him to be distracted from the deep trauma that he is immersed in.

Stephen gets more calls from Katie. She begins to use him to pick up her drugs and to help out driving stolen goods. He wants to be used. He wants to be absorbed inside her world...he quickly becomes addicted to her and the lifestyle that she leads. It is a complete opposite of his former life. Everything is turned upside down.

He has been given 'leave' from work for an unspecified time 'until you're better' was how they approached the matter.

Stephen is still living at his friend's place and doing his best to keep his new life private. He makes arrangements to see his children.

In just a few weeks he has changed appearance, mannerisms and behaviour. What started off as a form of escapism into someone else's world to try and forget the reality of his own has quickly turned into a form of addiction and obsession.

Several things are happening at once in his life. He has actually fallen in love with a prostitute. The depth of his pain from the marital breakdown is so deep that he has had to re-invent himself to deal with the situation. And, on top of all of this he has discovered that the level of excitement that he is now experiencing is taking him on a journey into a previous unknown world that is full of intrigue.

Stephen and Katie were two extremes just a few weeks ago, but it is her world that he is drawn towards. He is even able to cope with her sexual encounters to finance the lifestyle. Everything moves so much quicker in this new world. Things are becoming much larger than any life. They are becoming surreal.

After years in the legal profession Stephen finds it interesting observing the other side, and before long he is effectively on the wrong side of the law.

Katie has learned how to steal cars, break into property, make effective use of stolen credit cards and line up 'insider raids' with a network of contacts who communicate solely by way of mobile phone and text messages.

Stephen is living purely on the buzz and adrenaline of their actions.

Things change suddenly when a shoplifting episode goes wrong and she is caught by security. Stephen's efforts and advice don't amount to much in the circumstances and Katie is sentenced to 3 months in Peterborough Prison, although she is only likely to spend 6 weeks there.

Stephen finds time to reflect. He talks to his friend Phil one night and tells him about the last few months.

Phil tells Stephen that his wife's affair has finished and she realises what a mess she has made of everyone's life. He suggests to Stephen that he and Deborah should think about the future and what is best for the children.

Stephen and Deborah arrange to meet one night for dinner after Phil and his wife say they will look after the children for the evening.

They meet at a restaurant and it soon becomes evident that their respective actions tell them so much about their real lives that they were either unable to see or own up to before. During their amicable and friendly discussion each of them realises that they were living in a pre-conditioned way for many years and that since they had been unleashed they now saw things from a different perspective.

No matter how crazy each of their actions had been they came to the decisions they made on impulse. They had allowed their decision making to come from somewhere within, influenced only by their natural requirements and needs as human beings.

Stephen and Deborah agree to another meeting to talk, but the actions of the last few months have changed them both...Deborah

would like to keep the family unit together but Stephen is unable to relate to things in his 'previous life'.

Katie comes out of prison but has ripped off a dealer and she suggests to Stephen that they go under cover for a few days until things cool.

They spend 4 days and nights in a secret hideaway. A basement beneath a shop that they turn into a miniature film set. It is here that they discover body parts in a freezer. Katie is quite unconcerned by this and even Stephen comes to terms with it.

They 'furnish' their new home by taking things off a skip and by way of a few break-ins. In just 24 hours they create 'a home'. This environment is another merging of the tantalising mix of part reality part fantasy.

They have 'dinner' together in a room lit by 200 candles, during conversations Katie talks of her past which she has rarely made any mention of. She reveals the deep pain of her baby being put into care. She cries for the first time. Stephen can see in an instant that they are both in this thing to escape, and they have become deeply connected.

Close character studies begin to emerge, the viewers may well be asking questions of themselves by now as the film attempts to look at the way many of us just exist rather than live.

But are there any real alternatives for many of us? Some of us never question the 24 seven of dull repetitive jobs, dumbed down television and media, a continual pattern of the ordinary and uninspiring data that is force fed that turns us into cannon fodder pulp - and programmes our minds to purchase and possess things that we don't really require.

There are 'docu' style insets during the film that illustrate the blandness of everyday living.

Throughout proceedings Katie continues with her drug intake, but Stephen stays clean.

Eventually time runs out for Katie, she turns a car over one night and ends up in intensive care. Stephen finds out 2 days later. He is at her bedside and relives a flood of imagery from their time together in the way that pictures of your life may flash by in the moment before death.

After it is confirmed that there is no hope for her they turn off the life support machine.

Stephen arranges Katie's funeral. It becomes a visual and emotional cornerstone of the film.

Stephen enters a deep depression that eventually requires hospital care.

He is visited by Deborah on a number of occasions.

After a few months he is released back into society, but starts to get 'flashbacks' of Katie.

He ends up in a lonely bed-sit. He fights for personal survival and to get his life back on track. Eventually he starts to get back on track....and begins to see his children again.

One night he returns to the Red Light District where he first saw Katie, and sees someone else lurking in the shadows.....

Central Characters

There are two central characters in the film. In addition each of the characters has a friend.

Stephen McKenna, is a 41 year old solicitor, married to Deborah for 12 years. They have two children, Thomas is 9 and Emily 4. Stephen comes from a family who have a long legal background. He is originally from Cheshire but has settled to live in Suffolk. He lives comfortably in a 4 bedroom detached 'executive style' house in Woodbridge.

Stephen is extremely well spoken and almost always of smart attire, at least until his liaisons with Katie begin. He is of high intellect and well travelled.

Katie is 21, and has been involved in prostitution since she was 17. She is a heroin addict. She left home (also from Cheshire) when she was 16. She has 'lived' in about 50 different places in the last 4 years. She is an 'expert' in breaking into cars / property / shoplifting. She has a 4 year old daughter 'Amy' who was taken from her by the social services as a baby.

Katie is about as streetwise as anyone can be, attractive and supremely confident. She is fearless and reckless. She has grown accustomed to living on the edge and needs the thrill of it. She has knowledge of credit card fraud.

Stephen has one close friend he confides in - Phil, a fellow solicitor and squash partner.

Katie has a friend who leads a similar lifestyle to herself. Kelly is 23 and spends her time between working the streets and stealing which leads to short sentences at Peterborough Prison.

Locations / Backdrop / Scenery

The film is set in the East of England...against a backdrop of neon lit garage forecourts, alleyways on housing estates, run down b&b's, off season holiday resorts, squats, portacabins, behind the scenes in fast food joints, cafes, industrial estate warehousing, market towns, supermarket carparks, interiors of tattooists / taxi firms / fruit machine mentality / places that depict the raw underbelly of British sub-culture - it's not Blair's Britain, it never was, everything grows from the streets.

I want the viewer to understand that the subject matter that may usually be associated with our cities covers the entire country. Hooded youths in their thousands blanket the entire nation in a sophisticated and intricate network that is so vast it is almost unimaginable.

There is an enormous black economy underworld operating through every waking hour - every waking day. Christmas day too, it never relents. It swirls around us in our cities, towns, on the urban plains and in rural Britain. It is total and beyond the penetration of police or government.

There is a gradual shift in cultural and social evolution that grows every single day going unnoticed by a majority of the population, too busy watching games shows and living their own form of junk lifestyle without even realising it.

Ultimately it all leads to a growing strata of paranoia and dysfunctional / debased living habits / standards.

Presentation Document

A presentation document that was A3 landscape and consisted of about 8 pages of text and images from 'Dirty Blonde at the Cash Machine' was sent out to a few London based film production companies to see what, if any, feedback there might be.

It's quite difficult getting anything looked at and it was at least encouraging to find that several people had taken the time to read what I had sent.

SPARKFILMS

Here is the basic feedback that came from two companies and a few individuals in August 2006.

That they resonated with the depth of the two main characters.

The basic storyline to the film was interesting but not ground-breaking.

As a writer I was virtually unknown in the film world.

There was limited box office appeal for similar subject matter.

A rough idea of the production costs for the project were in the region of £600,000 to £850,000 with no guarantee of recouping the investment after screenings, possible television broadcasting and DVD sales.

Despite this fairly lukewarm and expected response there was a 50 / 50 split from those who responded that the film might be worth making from an artistic and social point of view if not a financial one.

I continued to write parts of the script but up until now, I have never re-presented it to any third parties.

Having given a few people in London a taste of Ipswich streetlife in August, I wondered what their reaction might be to the drama that unravelled just a few months later.

Perhaps it was as well that the part about the abductions by an Eastern European gang were not included in the initial outline story.

Either way, and in the most extraordinary circumstances, the film idea that I had been unable to take any further at that stage would be partly played out on dramatic television news and in a series of subsequent documentaries a few months and a few years later.

SKY NEWS

Reflections

The scene in Ipswich, pre-murders

There must have been a lot of people from different walks of life who got caught up in The Suffolk Murders in different ways. I would be the only person though who had released a book with its origins on the streets of Ipswich and written a draft filmscript based in the town's Red Light Area just a few months before the tragic events unfolded.

For all the work that I did it only represented my take on things. These were personal observations translated into a number of different art forms. In some ways it does not seem right to produce art from a series of murders when there are family members and people who are looking for closure. But at least much of that 'art' was already produced or existed as a form of 'work in progress' months before Steve Wright went on a killing spree.

At the heart of my writing was an empathy about the plight of the girls who get caught up in prostitution. I wanted to express hidden aspects of their lives that might enlighten people to their desperation.

I do not claim to be the only person who wrote about the lives of these girls with any degree of compassion, but if there were others expressing a similar sentiment then I was not aware of it at the time. At least that has changed to some degree since December 2006, and there can be no doubt that the BBC drama 'Five Daughters' has played its part.

During my appearances on television at the time of the murders, and in particular with Sky News, I was allowed the opportunity to speak about these girls and their lives with some tenderness, and it was a very pleasant surprise to hear that it had been well received in some quarters, although I'm sure, not all.

Although some parts of the media were criticised for some of their reporting from Ipswich I was very grateful that I was given every opportunity to speak up in my own way for the girls.

The Lives that Should Have Been Saved

Like many others I wondered if all of the girls were properly protected in early December 2006. I don't think much could have been done in respect of Tania Nicol or Gemma Adams, and possibly not in the case of Anneli Alderton.

It just seemed to me that over the weekend of Saturday 2nd December - when the second body was discovered, it was even more apparent that the girls on the streets of Ipswich were putting their lives on the line to get their drugs. If there was ever a time when some really lateral and extreme thinking and planning was required then this seemed like the time.

I expressed some ideas I had about the situation on the streets with some people at Sky News studio in Isleworth after a live interview. My thinking was that the entire Red Light Area should have been put under surveillance. I even suggested that the police allow the army to assist...in fact I went even further and mentioned MI5.

When lives are being taken in this way you should stop at nothing and do everything in your power or beyond it to save people. My words were not lost on one gentleman at Sky News who encouraged me to translate my thoughts to Suffolk Police.

A few days later, I think perhaps on a Saturday morning, I managed to get in front of the police at Martlesham Heath - home of Suffolk Constabulary and run through the army surveillance thing. At least they gave me the opportunity to speak but I didn't get the kind of eye contact or reaction that suggested in any way that I was making sense.

Thinking back on that now I wonder if I was making sense. Here I was as a small time writer and former client to some of the girls in Ipswich suggesting to a police force with hundreds of officers at their disposal that they needed the army to come in.

The way I saw my idea working was something like this. I imagined there were maybe 6 to 8 girls maximum still working on the streets. Surely it was possible to have people hidden every 50 metres watching their every move, taking all vehicle registrations, listening in to all conversations with a series of radio mics and so on.

This could have been done with people hidden in gardens, office buildings, rooftops, private cars and in a number of places dotted around the perimeter of the area.

Was I letting my ideas run away with me? Did my ideas border on forms of entrapment that might have legal implications further on down the line? One thing for sure, the police never said much in response, in fact, I don't recall them saying anything at all really.

Still, at least I had downloaded my strategy...for what it was worth, and unless that gentleman in London had prompted me, I may never have done so.

Give the Girls the Drugs

And then, more than three years later, it dawned on me. There really was a much simpler way of saving lives than my army deployment. I can't say that I thought of it myself, and nor did I know if the police ever considered at the time.

Surely, the way to save the lives of Paula Clennell, Annette Nicholls and very nearly Tracey Russell would have been to give those girls and a few others that were still out on the streets the drugs directly. That way there was no need for any girls to have been out there - or the other thing that somehow didn't register with me at the time, was to arrest any girl working on the streets for soliciting, and get them somewhere safe, and if need be, give them the drugs then.

Was it me that was missing something here or was it the police and authorities?

As I was later to discover the idea of giving money to the girls directly had already been implemented in some way, but even this had failed to keep some of those girls off the streets, so I still wonder how that all unfolded at the time.

While I am discussing this I think it is important to state that some members of the police and authorities treated those girls with extreme care, kindness and consideration, way beyond their call of duty.

Somehow though, I always felt that Paula Clennell and Annette Nicholls should still be with us today.

The only girl I knew of the five was Anneli Alderton, but the tragic story of Paula Clennell was the one that upset me the most. I remember her voice so clearly in a television interview when she was still on the streets in her final hours, saying 'I need the money'...there must have been a lot of us who wish we could have given her a hug that night. We never got the chance.

Only during revelations in the BBC drama Five Daughters did I start to understand more about Paula's life and the three daughters that she had to give up. Although the focus of my work is on events in Ipswich Paula's story is repeated all over the country and beyond. It's too sad to contemplate.

Back to the murders. I don't think it was ever made clear if the girls had taken or been given an amount of drugs that may have sedated them or incapacitated them in some way. There were suggestions of this in the press at the time and there were further hints during the trial, but as far as I'm aware the toxicology reports were unable to confirm this and it has never been fully explained. Nothing ever suggested that Steve Wright had access to drugs or kept them at his property.

As for the causes of death...Tania Nicol, Gemma Adams and Annette Nicholls were inconclusive. Anneli Alderton died from asphyxiation and Paula Clennell from compression of the neck. All this leaves many questions unanswered.

It is my guess that there was some degree of asphyxiation in each of the deaths. It is also my belief that each of the girls may have met their deaths in the Ford Mondeo belonging to Steve Wright.

Black bin liners?

As far as I know not a single item of clothing or the girls belongings was ever found by the police. There were reports of shoes being found near a garage and some clothes washed up on the banks of the River Orwell, but I don't think there was any link between these finds and the five girls.

My thoughts at the time were that the killer may simply have disposed of the belongings by putting them in black bin liners and placed them either in wheelie bins or perhaps even with his own refuse. I wondered if some of the items may have been disposed of at or near Hintlesham Hall - located close to the first two deposition sites, and suggested this to the police at the time.

There would have been a considerable amount collected from the five girls, as they would have been dressed for winter, possessions would also have included any bags and their contents. There may have been some amounts of cash, mobile telephones and cigarettes.

SKY NEWS

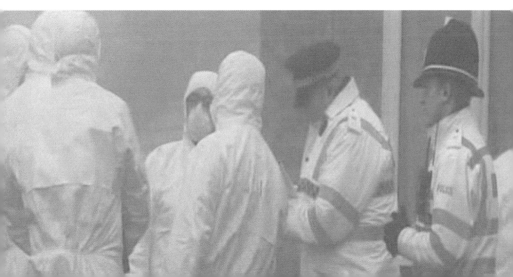

Some people suggested at the time that the items may have been burned or buried. I just thought they may have been put in bin liners and either thrown away around the time the bodies were abandoned or stored or hidden somewhere, and there still has to be a slight chance they may be found years later.

It did seem from the reports that I heard at the time that extensive searches were made at refuse sites that were linked to the removal of domestic and industrial areas that may have been connected to the movements of the killer.

Tracey Russell and the 'Mystery Red Blanket'

It was only after the trial that former Ipswich working girl Tracey Russell was able to speak to the national press about her encounters with the convicted murderer Steve Wright. I found it very strange that she was not asked to give evidence by the prosecution. The bulk of the evidence during the trial was scientific and there were times when I wondered if it would even bring about a conviction.

Tracey mentions that Steve Wright had been a client of hers for 3 years and not just the few months since Wright had moved into the red light area. She stated that sex always took place on the bed and not on a reflective jacket or anything else placed on the

SKY NEWS

floor. She refutes the claim that Wright ever removed condoms with gloves as was alluded to as part of his defence. She states that sex acts took place both at Wright's home and in his car.

Her account of liaisons with Steve Wright is very different from his version and far more believeable. As far as I could see she was able to eradicate a number of grey areas with her key information.

Perhaps the most graphic part of her account is when she mentions a red picnic blanket that was laid on the back seat of Wright's car. There were many references during the trial to the red fibres from something that I had thought might have been a cover or throw from a sofa at 79 London Road.

It was suggested that this red covering may have been used to wrap the bodies in and carry them to the deposition sites - just like the girls' clothes and belongings it was never found. Tracey's explanation of the 'mystery blanket' crystalised the red fibre issue, or at least, offered a reasonable explanation.

Pinned down on the bed in a Near Death Experience

Tracey was picked up by Wright on or around December 14th 2006, this was after all five bodies had been recovered. How this happened with police and roadblocks nearby is anyone's guess. She is taken back to 79 London Road where shortly after arriving she is pinned down naked on the bed, perhaps in the final moments of her life.

Suddenly there is the sound, possibly from a car door, and Steve Wright releases his grip and orders Tracey to quickly get dressed, even helping her. She hurries down the stairs and leaves by the front door. It would seem from her account that this was the one and only time she would leave by the front door.

As far as I know it was never established what that sound was that may have saved Tracey's life. She seemed to think it might be Wright's partner Pamela returning home unexpectedly from work. As far as the time that this may have occurred, Ms Russell mentions in her account to newspapers that Wright would usually trawl the red light area sometime after 11pm.

Tracey Russell told the police about her almost fatal experience with Wright but for some reason, the prosecutors chose not to use any of this at the trial. I'm not sure if during police interviews Ms Russell had mentioned the red picnic blanket, it may not have seemed relevant to her at the time of questioning, and perhaps the red fibre issue was not at the top of the police list of questioning. In fact at the time, it may have counted for very little.

If the prosecution were to go down the scientific route in the way that they did, then Tracey's observations may have helped the jury and millions of members of the public who were following proceedings in court. Tracey seemed more than capable of sharpening up a number of blurred edges.

I wonder if Pamela Wright was ever asked about a red blanket or cover? It also makes me wonder how Steve Wright had managed to keep his frequent visits to the red light area - especially since 2003, a secret from his partner Pamela Wright.

It was also reported that Steve Wright was known to cruise the red light area in a woman's wig, a PVC skirt and high heels. Perhaps Steve Wright enjoyed cross dressing too while at home. Wright seemed to have several strange habits, perhaps his partner just accepted them.

Washing Machines in the Middle of the Night

If the prosecution thought the sound of washing machines being used after midnight and a car being cleaned at strange hours was worth bringing to the attention of the jury, then surely, an account of Tracey Russell's near death experience was worthy of mention.

Something else that Tracey mentions - the last time she saw Steve Wright his hands were covered in residue. A quote from an interview published in The Daily Record on Feb 22, 2008 reveals the following 'He had white on his hands. He looked like he had been messing about with cement'. Perhaps this means nothing at all, or it could mean that he has concreted the girl's clothing and other evidence into the ground somewhere.

I came across a piece in a book by Paul Harrison entitled 'Hunting Evil - Inside the Ipswich Serial Murders' published in 2008 that confused me. Someone who uses the name of 'Lisa' - but to my mind must be Ms Russell, is describing the night when she could have been the sixth victim. From page 188 of this book I quote - 'This time he took me to his house in London Road which he had never done before'. The rest of her account of that night with Wright is more or less in accordance with her subsequent press interviews. Perhaps something had become lost in translation here.

The Fibre Evidence - Red Acrylic

After an in-depth search on the internet I managed to find a report that was compiled by Ray Palmer - Consultant Forensic Scientist. This was in a PDF format and looked like some kind of presentation to the police or media that gave an analysis of the forensic evidence under the title of 'The Ipswich Killings'.

In actual fact, as I was later to discover, Ray Palmer's 'report' turned out to be part of a presentation he gave at the Trace Evidence Symposium at Clearwater Beach in Florida in August 2009.

My initial interest focused on the red acrylic samples, and although they seemed very small in number and were only detected on Anneli Alderton, Paula Clennell and Gemma Adams I began to realise the significance of these findings.

After watching the actual presentation Ray Palmer made at The Symposium via an online video recording I was able to understand far more about the vital collection of fibres that are gathered to be used as evidence.

We are always hearing about DNA, and without it, Wright may never have been caught, but when the fibre issues are dealt with in minute detail a far more in depth picture begins to emerge and it was becoming much clearer to see how the prosecution were gradually building their case.

I began to see the crime from a different perspective after studying some of the fibre evidence, beginning with the places where the bodies of the girls were found namely, firstly in water - Nicol and Adams, and secondly on land - Alderton, Nicholls and Clennell.

In the case of Nicol, her body had been in water for just over 5 weeks and that of Adams for just over two weeks. For those that were found on the land, the length of exposure to the elements was Alderton 7 days, Nicholls 4 days and Clennell 2 days.

Exposure to the Wind and the Rain

These timings and conditions would clearly mean that it would be far easier to gather information in respect to fibre collection from the three girls who were discovered in woodland areas. It also has to be taken into account that for each day of exposure to the wind and rain the chances of gathering fibre samples diminishes.

I need to jump forward a little here to the number of fibres that were found on each girl and used in the trial as evidence against Steve Wright. It has to be remembered that the following figures only include a small proportion of the overall readings taken and that these stats only pertain to the link between the victims and the accused.

After the bodies of Nicol and Adams had been in water for the length of time stated it was incredible to think that anything at all could be found as fibre evidence, but as it was there were

22 examples from Nicol and 14 from Adams. The land readings reflect the duration of exposure to the elements in a clearer way - Alderton 7 days and 33 fibre examples used as evidence, Nicholls 4 days - 60 examples and Clennell 2 days - 48 examples.

Once again I should point out that the sum total of these findings - I make it 177, was only a small proportion of the overall amount of fibre readings that were collected. There is then a process to identify each fibre and it's origin. Information is compiled that begins to put the fibres into groups that will begin to describe if they may have come from clothing, blankets, car seats and so on.

The findings that were collected in the Ipswich case consisted of a huge number of readings that could not initially be linked to any particular people or environments. But once they are recorded there is an opportunity to match them to any other information that may be collected by DNA or by other means as the case progresses.

Yellow Fluorescent Polyester

Included in the huge amount of information that was being processed were such descriptions as 'Green - Blue Viscose', 'Yellow Fluorescent Polyester' and 'Blue Polyester'. I should imagine that after years of experience and study of fabric components the forensic teams start to get an idea of where the fabrics come from - maybe starting with defining if something has been taken from a cushion or a sock for instance, or from a carpet or a tee shirt.

Once the police and forensic teams had established a DNA profile for Wright from the bodies of Alderton, Clennell and Nicholls, they were then able to scrutinise his property at London Road and collect items of clothing for example that would begin to match up to the samples they had collected from the bodies. So, going back to the 'Green - Blue Viscose' for instance, this matched a pair of Wright's gloves, the 'Yellow Fluorescent Polyester' was from his reflective jacket and the 'Blue

Polyester' was a match for some Umbro tracksuit bottoms that Wright owned.

Perhaps the most dramatic find was a single carpet fibre from the footwell of Steve Wright's Mondeo that had somehow survived over 5 weeks in the hair of Tania Nicol - despite being immersed in the running current of a stream for most of that time. I should add that the defence could rightly claim that this carpet fibre could also have come from thousands of other vehicles. I think the relevance of this particular find, was that for it to be lodged in the hair of Tania Nicol, some considerable force may have been required.

At the end of Ray Palmer's presentation in Florida there is an opportunity for the audience to ask questions. The question that stood out for me, actually it was more his answer, was when some-one asked Palmer where he thought the murders took place. Palmer thought all the murders would have taken place in Wright's Mondeo. That would have made things far simpler when depositing the bodies - and represents a lot less effort than moving bodies from his house to the car in the early hours.

Toxicology results and Hints the Girls were Sedated

There seemed to be a theory in some circles in early reports that the girls may have been even more under the influence of substances than one would normally expect. This made me think that they had been given a fix of some kind very shortly before death which could possibly have made them even more vulnerable. My thinking around this time was that one of their regular clients may also have been in a position to obtain the drugs in advance of picking up the girls.

At this stage of events I wondered if their minder and friend Tom Stephens may have had this kind of opportunity. Eventually, I tended to discount that line of thought - but I should imagine it was something the police may have been working on too.

During the trial Pathologist Dr Nathanial Cary told the jury that the women may have been too intoxicated to resist attack. By 'too intoxicated' I was never sure if he meant that their normal drug intake around that time was such that they may have been unable to resist attack, or that he was implying they were given something 'extra' - so to speak.

My interest in the 'extra' had come about by a heroin addict mentioning something that was going around in Ipswich at the time that could 'knock you out'. As it happened, I never got any more information to support this, but it had painted a picture in my mind of how these girls may have met their end.

Dr Cary described the causes of death and aspects of how the women were found. Up until this point very little of this information would have been in the public domain. His findings would certainly introduce clues as to how these women died, but to this day, there is no definitive explanation of the exact mode of murder or where the murders actually took place. It is possible though from Dr Cary's findings to understand far more about how these women died than it had been pre-trial.

The jury heard how heroin can have the effect of a sedative. He described how brain opiate receptors would be influenced by the drug and that taking heroin could cause sleepiness, semi-consciousness or even unconsciousness, depending on the dose.

Gemma Adams resting place was in a brook at Hintlesham near Ipswich where she was discovered on Saturday, December 2nd, 2006. She was naked and had been in water for a duration of just over two weeks. Ms Adams was under the influence of morphine - derived from heroin intake at the time of death, there were also traces of methadone.

Her death appears to have come from compression of the neck or smothering, or perhaps a combination of both. It was also stated that there was hyperventilation of the lungs that would be consistent with fighting for breath. A haemorrhage in the left eye consistent with asphyxiation was also present. Despite this explanation her actual cause of death was unascertained.

Tania Nicol's body was found by police divers at Copdock Mill on Friday, December 8th, 2006. Tania had been in water for just under 6 weeks. She was significantly intoxicated after taking heroin - stated as 'very high levels of morphine indicative of heroin ingestion'. She had bruising to her right inner arm and there was an injury to the back of her knee that suggested some force may have been used from behind. Tania suffered damage to the thyroid cartilage and tissue damage close to the windpipe. Suggestions were that the cause of death came from compression or squeezing of the neck. When considering the carpet fibre that was found in Tania's hair it seems as though she may have met her death in the footwell of Wright's Ford Mondeo.

'Subtle Asphyxiation' - but many Injuries to the Body

Anneli Alderton was discovered in woodland at Nacton on Sunday, December 10th, 2006. Anneli's corpse had laid in the woods for seven days. She was under the influence of heroin and cocaine at the time of her death. There was also a mixture created by the consumption of cocaine and alcohol present. Her cause of death was described as 'subtle asphyxiation'. When reading through some of the injuries she endured it was difficult to understand any-thing of a subtle nature. Injuries included damage to both eyes, her left upper lip, a graze on the chin, bruising on the left arm and left elbow, bruises and scratches to the front upper left shin, and two grazes to the upper right shin.

None of these injuries was thought to have been caused by the movement of her body. Additionally there were further injuries recorded that included purple bruising at the opening of the vagina, bruising to a neck muscle and bleeding to the side of her voice box that was consistent to compression or impact. All this seems to add up to compression of the mouth and neck or a com-bination of both. In another statement the term 'sleeper hold - to block the airwaves' was used.

There were graphic descriptions about the placement of the body. Anneli was found naked in a cruciform position with arms out-stretched, her left palm facing up and her right palm facing down. Her right leg was outstretched while her left leg was slightly bent at the knee. Her hair was poised 'almost symmetrically straight up'. One of the most unusual observations relating to her body was that it was 'dark brown in colour'. I think the reason for this dramatic discolouration was explained by the residue from the falling vegetation above.

As I had known Anneli I was asked by the police if I would be prepared to identify her body. I agreed to this but as things turned out I was not called upon to do so.

Annette Nicholls was found in Levington on Tuesday, December 12th, 2006. She had been there for 4 days. Annette was intoxicated with morphine while methadone and cocaine were also traced. She had mud on her feet suggesting that she may have been dragged towards her resting place by her perpetrator. As with Anneli Alderton, Ms Nicholls was placed in a cruciform position. There were scratches on her body that may have been caused when she moved through vegetation. The scratches were detected on her right breast, spine and lower back. Once again there seemed to be a reason of death due to compression of the neck associated with 'minimum trauma'.

Paula Clennell's body was also found in Levington on Tuesday, December 12th, 2006. Paula's body was discovered just two days after her disappearance. Morphine from ingested heroin was present in Ms Clennell's body, as was the evidence of cocaine. Reason for death seemed to point towards 'compression of the neck by the hands or the crook of an arm'. Paula suffered injuries to her right shoulder and right collarbone. Circular bruising on the neck suggested a form of struggle or forceful blow.

The bodies of Adams and Nicol that were found in water were thought to have been dropped from Burstall Bridge. This may have meant that Steve Wright only had to carry or drag the bodies over the course of a few metres. The bodies of Alderton, Clennell and Nicholls that were left in wooded areas by the side of the road may have required a little more effort as they were placed between about 5 and 15 metres from the roadside.

79 London Road, Ipswich

This is a house I have viewed from the front on a number of occasions. I was tempted to revisit the property for the purpose of this book and take a quick walk down the driveway to get an idea of the layout behind and to the side. After reading that those living nearby are none too keen on tourists I relented.

The purpose of my survey would have been to try and ascertain how Steve Wright may have moved the bodies, that is, assuming that the girls were murdered at this address and moved to the deposition sites in Wright's Mondeo. After a little homework that included viewing a very good front on photograph of the property showing the drive to the right hand side, the rear car park and a partial perimeter fence, it looked possible that Wright may have parked his car at the rear of the property.

In addition to this an image from Google Earth showed the outline of the back of the house and a garden had also been mentioned by Pamela Wright at some stage.

From accounts by Tracey Russell and some of the other working girls it seemed that they entered and exited through a patio door at the back of the property when sexual transactions with the accused took place. I am having to assume a few things here, perhaps in the way that the police may have done, but I am beginning to get a picture of an incredibly difficult, and high risk task in moving bodies to a car from the property.

Carrying or dragging a body through rooms, down a staircase, opening doors at the house and the doors or boot of a car would require at least several instances when the body had to be placed on the ground. Perhaps with all of this taken into account by the police, the possible accomplice theory was born.

The notion that two people may have been involved in these murders was to continue before, during and after the trial. At any time someone could easily have seen or heard something from an adjoining property, but it would seem no one ever did.

I noticed how the jury seemed to be whisked past the property in a vehicle during the trial. I'm not sure if they would have learned too much from this. A look around the inside of the house and an opportunity to examine the garden, drive and rear car park may have been more beneficial. It seems, from reports I read later, that the jury declined the opportunity to view the property and the surrounds at closer quarters.

There is something else I should mention here. It was reported that it was common for Steve Wright to park his car on the drive at the front of the house, but I suppose there is always the possibility that he may have used the side drive and rear car park on occasions when he was perhaps trying to shield any girls he was taking back there.

While on the subject of 79 London Road I have learned recently that Pam Wright, partner of Steve Wright, had suspicions that he was using the services of prostitutes nearby soon after they moved to their new address.

Murders and Body Depositions may have Occurred at High Speed

CCTV footage at the trial indicates that Wright was seen driving out of Ipswich at around 1.40am on the nights Nicol and Alderton was last seen. It was assumed that he was taking the bodies to their resting place. Perhaps each of the bodies was taken to the deposition sites after 1.30am.

As Wright was reported to have trawled the red light area after 11pm a possible time zone for the activities of picking up the women, murdering them and off loading their bodies at the deposition sites may all have occurred in a time frame of just an hour or so. I always thought that his activities would have occurred very quickly.

Wright had stated at the trial that he would either have sex with a prostitute in his car or in his flat. When bringing home women to his address in London Road he seems to have followed a procedure where he would drive to the back of the property and enter the premises through a patio door. He also described how when a prostitute was leaving his property, he would check at the front to see if it was all clear for her to leave, and if it was, she would walk out of the front door.

Since Wright lived in the very heart of the red light area and the girls who left his house in the way he describes would not have to walk very far to continue their business. Several sites for the murders scenes have been considered by the police and forensic teams, and it might just be possible from studying what Wright says during his statements in court, or maybe, reading between the lines, where the girls perished.

Referring again to the account of working girl Tracey Russell, when she described hurriedly leaving by the front door on the occasion that she may have become the sixth victim - it did imply that to leave by the front door was unusual in her case, and it sounds as though she may have left through the back patio doors normally. It seems she must have visited 79 London Road several times.

Wright had indicated that he had seen 12 different girls between moving in to his London Road address up until the time of his arrest nearly three months later. It also seems from his account that he only saw one of those girls on more than one occasion. If it was Tracey who he saw twice, then her account leaves rea-

son for doubt. Of the 13 transactions Wright admits to over the time period there seems to be a fairly even split between escorting this women back to his home and having sex with them in his car.

Perhaps Ms Russell may have been referring to Wright's previous address in Bell Close as she always indicated that Wright had been one of her clients for about 3 years.

After listening to Wright's account of his activities with each of those young women on the last night of their lives it may well be that Nicol and Adams were murdered in his Mondeo and Alderton, Clennell and Nicholls were killed at his home. Other than that I agree with Ray Palmer, the fibre expert who thought all the murders occurred in Wright's car.

No DNA from Tom Stephens found on the bodies

Dr Peter Hau, the forensic scientist giving evidence at the trial of Steve Wright was able to enlighten the jury and the public with his findings regarding the bodies of Anneli Alderton, Annette Nicholls and Paula Clennell. Dr Hau made a very firm point that no DNA from first suspect Tom Stephens was traceable on any of the bodies. It was important to establish the absence of any possible link to Stephens as some people were of the opinion that he may have been 'the second man'. As with the fibre evidence Stephens had nothing to link him in any way to the bodies of the women.

The only 'full profile DNA' found on these women had come from defendant Steve Wright. It was interesting to learn from Dr Hau that some people shed more DNA than others, such as people who sweat a lot. The DNA that was found on Anneli Alderton from Wright was described as 'body rich fluid', this may refer to saliva, sweat or semen. There were also low level DNA profiles found on the bodies from unknown persons.

It was surprising to hear that it was quite possible for someone to carry out a murderous attack without leaving any trace of DNA.

The DNA from semen that was found on and in Steve Wright's gloves was to play a major part in the court proceedings. In his defence Wright had stated that he removed condoms with a glove as he found it 'distasteful' - it cannot be very often that someone has needed to remove a condom with a gloved hand. His version of events suggest that he either wore gloves while engaging in illicit acts or put them on immediately afterwards. I'm not sure if anyone believed that.

There may yet be an appeal in this case. I learned that it was the intention to get a second opinion on all the scientific evidence that was gathered and for it to be sent to scientists in the USA for further in-depth analysis. Several attempts to process this seem to have stalled.

Should an appeal ever transpire it might require 6 or 7 prostitutes who had sex with Wright between early October and the time of his arrest on Tuesday 19th December 2006 to come forward as witnesses. Wright had stated at the trial that he had sex with at least 12 prostitutes in this time period, this includes the five he killed and seems to average about one encounter a week.

Gloves to Remove Condoms

I'm sure those women would remember if Wright ever wore gloves to remove condoms, and if he was actually speaking the truth it would bring far more substance to any appeal. Perhaps for this reason, or something like it, nothing as yet has been possible to consolidate. Apart from Tracey Russell in her post trial press interviews where she denounced Wright's glove habit, there were several other working girls who had described Wright as a regular punter, so one has to assume that Wright fabricated his story. It turned out to be a key part of the case, and his quite bizarre explanation must have helped the jury with their verdicts.

I'm not sure how the DNA evidence was presented during the trial. At the time of compiling this book I have been unable to see if anything diagrammatic exists anywhere. It would be helpful to establish precisely what levels of DNA were found, who the donors were - known or unknown, the areas on the bodies where the samples showed up, and anything that might give a better understanding of these findings. I don't doubt Dr Hau explained this in great detail at the time but perhaps I was spoilt by viewing the fibre presentation by Ray Palmer.

It seemed to me that 'swabbed areas' may have included the ankles of the victims, perhaps giving the slightest hint of how they may have been moved to their resting places.

I did make enquiries through Ipswich Crown Court to see if it might be possible to purchase the daily transcripts from the entire case. The transcripts are produced by a company in London and they charge somewhere around £120 a day for them to be processed. The entire case might cost about £3,000 to obtain, to do this you need written authority from the court.

The Ipswich Evening Star

After considering this I decided to gather as much information as I could by searching through the more than extensive coverage in the web archives of The Ipswich Evening Star. This at least proved a far more in-depth record of the trial and its findings than anything in the national press.

Back to the 'red fibre' issue. It seemed almost taken as read at the trial that Wright wrapped the bodies in the red picnic blanket that was identified by Tracey Russell as he dropped them from a bridge or carried them through vegetation. After hearing of the marks on the bodies it seems quite possible that he just lifted their naked corpses from the back of the car when discarding them. This would be more in keeping with each of the murders having taken place in the Mondeo.

What would be the point in covering a body in a blanket if you were wearing a reflective jacket?

The places where Wright dropped off the bodies in the dead of night would have been silent and deserted. Only a few seconds would have been required to drop each of the bodies from Burstall Bridge, and not much more in the case of Clennell and Nicholls at Levington. The only body that would have taken perhaps a little longer to deposit would have been that of Anneli Alderton in Nacton.

Wright was a fast and fearless worker. He worked alone. His killing spree was rapid and was virtually carried out on his own doorstep. It was the most extraordinary case and will long be remembered in British criminal history.

Michael Crimp - Crown Prosecution Service

During my trawls through the BBC News Suffolk Murders web pages I came across a video of Michael Crimp of the CPS speaking about the case and about Steve Wright. Towards the conclusion of the interview with a BBC journalist Mr Crimp speaks about a 'change' that occurred in Wright.

Here is what was said...'something in his (Wright's) life had changed in that he told the jury he had not used prostitutes in the street in Ipswich up until the beginning of October 2006, that he had previously used prostitutes in massage parlours, but something changed - that he started to use girls out on the street and within a very short period of time of him starting that five girls went missing'.

So had Steve Wright changed then? Actually no, not at all, and once again it was Tracey Russell who was to shed further light on this during her numerous and revealing press interviews after the trial. She states that she had seen Steve Wright in his capacity as a client since 2003 - long before he moved into the centre of the red light area in London Road.

So is Michael Crimp actually covering himself by saying 'in that he told the jury' etc...he is very careful to choose his words here, or maybe I am reading too much into it. Surely, with thousands of hours of interviews and statements in the system everyone working on the case was fully aware that Wright had used street prostitutes for many years before 2006.

Crimp's words imply that Wright's crimes only became possible once he had changed from using the services of girls in saunas and massage parlours after many years to street girls.

The Story Never Ends

Ipswich became the focal point of national and world media. It was just another English town with street prostitution and drug problems, but one thing made it different from other towns and cities in the UK, it was home to a serial killer.

I found myself writing some extra pages for this book when I heard of the death of Philippa Walker, and this in turn led to the realisation that the story surrounding the murders of five young women, three of whom were mothers, would live on forever in history and through future generations.

My involvement in events in Ipswich was firstly as a client and friend, then as a writer / researcher and later some kind of spokesperson and media consultant, then finally, as the writer of 'Ipswich Zero Six'.

The fleeting shadows that flickered in the twilight of Ipswich camouflaged stories of unimaginable pain and sorrow. As a small time writer I was drawn into this world for a short while in an attempt to gather information from the front line. It would be nice to think a little of what I have expressed connects with some people.

I think my real journey into this world began when I first saw Philippa, and perhaps its end was marked by the eventual news of her tragic death. So much happened in between. I felt compelled to write about it, and even if no one should ever read it, it was something I had to do.

Philippa Walker - 'Dirty Blonde at the Cash Machine'

I didn't expect to be including much about my 2006 book release that featured a working girl from Ipswich, but on the day of writing this I heard some very sad news.

After speaking to Brian Tobin of The Iceni Project in Ipswich I learned that Philippa Walker died of a suspected drug overdose in December 2009. Philippa was the central focus of a writing journey into the scene on the streets of Ipswich in the summer of 2005.

I wrote a series of poetic pieces of the times I spent with Philippa both as a client, then later, as someone at the end of the phone, sometimes at 4am, who would be only too pleased to drive 20 miles to see her and take her to get her drugs.

From 'Kamikaze Waitress'...'all your messages recorded and digitised, I listen to them through the night, sitting here waiting for you to call'...and that's just how it was.

From 'Dirty Blonde at the Cash Machine'...'It's been days now since I've been trailing in your shadows, taking you to vandalised payphones in the dead of night, listening to your anguished pleas, watching your moves in rear view mirrors'...I was only too pleased to share her airspace.

From 'Saving a Life'...'Always thought that I was born to save a life, yours maybe, some guardian angel appearing out of the mist by the Audi dealership in your darkest moment'...was it just poetic stuff?

Philippa was known to me as 'Katie' and I believe she later operated as 'Leah'. Whatever she was in life and whatever she did, Philippa made a very powerful impact on me and I would like to think she still lives on in some way in the pages in a book.

Millions of people learned of the deaths of the five girls in Ipswich but very few people would have known of the tragic death of Ms Walker. Philippa lived on just 3 years after the murders.

It does make one wonder what the life expectancy for those five girls may have been if a murderer had not gone on a killing spree.

It does seem quite possible that some of those girls may already have been too far down a path to self destruction, but we will never know.

When I wrote the film script for 'Dirty Blonde at the Cash Machine' - a working title that may well become 'Stephen and Katie' if the project should ever commence, the two main characters were based on 'Katie' and myself.

It is haunting now to revisit the script in which 'Katie' dies and the funeral is featured. In the film though, Katie does not die of a drug overdose, even though she is under the influence of drugs at the time of the accident that takes her life.

The news of Philippa's death triggered a flashflood of images and sounds. How could this seemingly invincible young woman's life possibly be extinguished?

I needed to find out about her last days, no matter how tragic they may have been and even went as far as obtaining a copy of her death certificate. It was almost as though I needed to see it in black and white to fully understand that she was gone.

Dying Alone in a Guest House

It was heartbreaking to learn that the time of her death was possibly Christmas Eve, 2009 and that the place where she silently left the world was just a room in a guest house in Ipswich.

Her date and place of birth is listed as 13th April, 1979 in Norwich, Norfolk.

There is no mention of an occupation. Her address is listed as the guest house where she died.

The cause of death is listed as 'Respiratory Depression' and a 'Combination of Opiates, Benzodiazepines and Alcohol', it makes for chilling reading.

There are few words on the certificate, each of them lays cold and lonely on the page. It is deeply upsetting. Despite the wildness and extreme nature of her lifestyle Philippa always seemed to be sprinkled in stardust.

I phoned the guest house where she died and learned of the circumstances of how she was found. It appears that Philippa had not been seen for several days and the proprietor of the establishment went to check on her by knocking on the door.

When there was no answer the room was checked from a window that was open. It was then that Philippa was seen slumped in a position that looked like she may have been sleeping. Philippa died alone and in silence in a room where she had been staying for just a few weeks.

Although the date of death is listed as Christmas Eve 2009 it is possible that her death occurred a day or so before. Philippa had virtually no possessions, the contents of her room fitting into nothing more than a single carrier bag.

One day perhaps her children will learn something of her life and her death. Despite the way that Philippa Mary Walker lived her life she possessed a unique combination of power and beauty, and despite once failing to save her from her demons, she was saving me from mine, and she could do it with just a kiss on the cheek. That's how incredible she was.

Killer in a Small Town · Channel 4

I was contacted in April 2008 - via photographer Stuart Nicholls, by Darlow Smithson, a television production company. They had seen a copy of Dirty Blonde at the Cash Machine, that Stuart had done the photography shoot on. They wondered if I might be able to contribute to a documentary about The Suffolk Murders that was scheduled for transmission on Channel 4.

Dirty Blonde at the Cash Machine had part of its origins on the streets of Ipswich. The actual title referred to a period of a few hours when I was driving one of the girls around in the dead of night to score drugs.

There were a number of similar pieces in the book which was a kind of ambient and poetic backdrop to the streets of England, and in particular, Ipswich at the time. The book was actually written through the late summer to autumn of 2005 and released in the spring of 2006...about 6 months before the girls started to go missing in Ipswich.

During the photoshoot for the book, which was actually shot in Luton, we attempted to replicate the visual backdrop that reflected the kind of world that had drawn me in - both in the capacity of a client initially and then as a place to gather reference and information at first hand for a number of writing projects.

Anyway, it seemed to have made some kind of impression on people who wanted to make a documentary and arrangements were put in place for me to have a meeting with the director Louise Osmond.

Hotel Meeting on the outskirts of Ipswich

The initial meeting occurred a couple of weeks later at a hotel on the outskirts of Ipswich. I took a considerable amount of material along to discuss and it was an interesting exchange.

I agreed to contribute and appear in the programme that was initially planned for 90 minutes I believe, but actually came out at 75 minutes.

The plan for the documentary, which was to be titled 'Killer in a Small Town', was to record first hand experiences from a number of people who were connected to the murders of the girls in different ways.

Those of us that appeared in the docu were filmed individually. Director Louise had mentioned some of the people who were taking part as things progressed, but I don't think any of us realised how in-depth and comprehensive the final production would be.

The production team were staying at a rented house in Suffolk and after a research period of several weeks when they had tracked down key members of the police, working girls, family members of the victims, and a number of other key people, a filming schedule was worked out.

As a small time film maker myself I found the process interesting and asked the occasional questions between the work that we did to get an idea of timings and so on.

From memory, I seem to think that somewhere between 25 and 30 days were required for the filming. Either way it was a considerable amount of work as the final cut demonstrated...and this perhaps only representing a small part of the many hours of footage and sound gathering that were collected.

Later on in the production process there would be weeks of work in the editing suite with a very considered voice over to link everything up.

Toyota Celica

Part of my contribution were a number of drives through the Red Light Area in my Toyota Celica that had an array of cameras mounted onto the bonnet. This process took several hours to assemble and was done in front of a passing and sometimes static audience in the car park of a restaurant in Ipswich town centre.

Having the cameras on board was only part of the process. There was an assortment of reflecting devices fitted in the car and when I was driving slowly around the streets director Louise Osmond was actually laying across the back seat tangled up in wires and bits of sound recording equipment.

Another part of my contributions took place in my home in Colchester. The set up of the camera angles and lighting took hours and was done with precision detail. Something that I said during filming was suitably dubbed over one of the driving sequences. 'The police had eye to eye contact with the killer - it couldn't have been any other way'.

Those words and their meaning were very important to me then and they are to this day. My take on things during the murders was that when the last two girls were taken from the streets there must have been such close police attention that they just had to have seen the killer at close quarters.

As it happened the police saw the killer at very close quarters during their inquiries as he was stopped in the Red Light Area and questioned. Having said that, I should imagine he was just one of hundreds.

I am not re-watching the 'Killer in a Small Town' DVD to assist me with this piece of writing as I just wanted to write about my most vivid recall from it and what really connected with me when watching it for the first time.

These are those key parts.

Alice, the sister of Paula Clennell speaking so openly and with raw honesty about something that many people could ever admit to.

Jade Reynolds, speaking about Annette Nicholls and a lovely day they spent together. Jade, that was beautiful.

Tracey Russell recalling the time she was at 79 London Road and how the sudden knock on the door may have saved her from being the 6th victim.

Stewart Gull describing the moment he was told of the DNA match on the last 3 bodies that was to bring about the arrest of Steve Wright and the end of the killings.

The filming I was involved with took place in May 2008.

'Killer in a Small Town' was broadcast in February 2009 on Channel 4 as part of 'Cutting Edge'.

The professional and dedicated people who were instrumental in this production were as follows -

Director / Producer: Louise Osmond.

Director of Photography: Jeremy Hewson.

Sound Recordist: Oliver Astles Jones.

Assistant Producer: Jamie Balment.

SPARKFILMS

Five Daughters - BBC 1

This was a three part drama written by screenwriter Stephen Butchard which was broadcast as one hourly programmes on consecutive nights in April 2010.

The objective was to concentrate more on the lives of the girls and the effects on their families and not to get too absorbed from the perspective of the usual police angle. As I understand it Stephen Butchard spent a few hours with those members of the families who agreed to participate.

Unlike 'Killer in a Small Town' I had no input as a contributor, even though it would have been very interesting to get involved in some way. There were however several aspects to the BBC drama that seemed to mirror references in the Channel 4 documentary.

Holloway Prison

I always knew it would be a little strange for me watching actors portray the lives of people that I either knew or had become familiar with and so it proved in the first episode. The opening shot of Jaime Winstone - playing Anneli Alderton, standing outside Holloway prison seemed to be an unconvincing part of the drama for me personally for quite an unusual reason.

Poor Ms Winstone seemed to be let down by the makeup people as she displayed an ill fitting wig. I soon learned that this was a fairly common observation and it is a real pity because after my early doubts things began to pick up.

Another part of the filming that was quite difficult for me to relate to was that most of the street scenes were shot in Bristol. With such powerful imagery of the streets of Ipswich x-rayed into my being it took a little getting used to...but I did get used to it as the characters of the girls and their stories began to unfold.

And just one more thing, we heard accents from all over the UK, virtually nothing from Suffolk, apart from Sean Harris playing Brian Tobin. Harris was one of the stars without a doubt.

These things said, from the many reviews I have read and hundreds of comments on sites like Digital Spy 'Five Daughters' was an overwhelming success. The drama managed to portray some very powerful insights into the harsh reality of the girls lives at that time.

Some of the stand out moments for me were.

The conversation between Brian Tobin representing the drug rehab centre at The Iceni Project in Ipswich with poor Paula Clennell, a meeting that seemed to take place just a few days before her death.

The shocking places some of those girls were prepared to take refuge and sleep in - in one instance an electricity cupboard.

The moment Juliet Aubrey playing Maire Alderton observes her daughter's corpse in the stillness and silence. This would have been a defining moment for actress Jaime Winstone playing Anneli Alderton.

The poetic writing of Annette Nicholls - although I understand that this was improvised by Butchard himself. Even so, it was a very powerful and moving part of the script.

The moment that the DNA links to Steve Wright are discovered.

The tracking of first suspect Tom Stephens in the final days when he has picked up a girl in the early hours from the Red Light District and is heading out towards one of the deposition sites.

'Nina' - in reality Tracey Russell, describing how her life was probably saved by that knock on the door at Steve Wright's home in London Road.

I watched every one of the 180 minutes over the three nights of

'Five Daughters' and found myself adding to the debate on Digital Spy over the following days.

Stephen Butchard's drama certainly helped me to join up a few more dots and explained a couple of things I had doubts about. It also prompted me to contact, and later meet up with the real Brian Tobin who actually lives in my home town of Colchester.

Afterthought

Having read through all this again before print I realise that my rapid writing style (that is intended to be raw and immediate) may be a little difficult to follow in places. Sorry if that is so.

Something else I would like to make a little clearer if possible is my guess at where the five young women may have met their deaths. Although it was known that Wright often took girls back to his home at 79 London Road, it seems more likely to me that he may simply have picked these five girls up off the street, taken them somewhere quiet, murdered them and disposed of their bodies in a very short timespan, perhaps as little as 30 minutes or so. I would be interested to hear from anyone with any ideas on this.

Christmas Day 2006

It is Christmas Day 2006.

I have just been to Ipswich to lay 5 white carnations in West End Road.

One each for Gemma Adams, Tania Nicol, Anneli Alderton, Annette Nicholls and Paula Clennell.

Last week at the same time I was on the same spot filming with Sky News. It was disappointing to see such a muted response. Flowers yes, but from no more than a dozen or so people.

A week on and it seems like my carnations might be the only addition.

Perhaps those that really do have any compassion for these poor girls really are in a tiny minority.

I decided to walk the perimeter of the Red Light District, thinking perhaps that others might do the same.

There was no one.

I noticed the hum of the air conditioning units in an office block that overlooks the area.

Things look much different here in daylight.

At night time this is a netherland of murky shadows tinged with a soft glow of orange street lighting.

I walked past 79 London Road, the house where the accused was living. I know these properties to be split into flats and bedsits. It is a world where people arrive then disappear and are never seen again.

There is still a white tent outside and the scaffold and

tarpaulin remain.

There are two police officers at the front of the property. One a WPC. They seem to be sharing some kind of joke.

At the back of the property I could see two other police officers.

The media have all gone. No need to tape the road off anymore.

I am struck by the quick return to normality. Just a few days ago there were media people here from all over the world.

Just as I was getting to the exit of this part of the zone something finally caught my eye.

In the garden of 111 London Road there were 5 candles burning brightly, protected from the breeze.

I wanted to knock on the door and thank those that lived there for their consideration, but it was Christmas morning and perhaps best if I did not disturb them.

I crossed Handford Road and went back to my car, passing the portable white information centre that the police had set up about 10 days ago.

The door was shut.

It seemed to be unmanned.

I would like to thank the following,

Philippa Walker.

Suffolk Constabulary
and police forces from across the UK.

Martin Brunt, Jeremy Thompson, David Crabtree
and all at Sky News.

Brian Tobin of The Iceni Project.

Mick Dickinson of Prontaprint Colchester.

Rosie Boycott.

The Kosovan taxi driver.

'MISS D', 'MISS K', 'MISS J',
'MISS L', and 'MISS R'.

Jacci Goldsmith.

Elizabeth Parnell.

Sangita Myska.

Louise Osmond, Jeremy Hewson,
Oliver Astles Jones & Jamie Balment.

The Open - for 'Lovers in the rain'.

The Ipswich Evening Star.

Tracey Russell.

All the team at Palladian Press.

They came into the world as angels.

Gemma Adams.

Tania Nicol.

Anneli Alderton.

Annette Nicholls.

Paula Clennell.

They left as angels.

And on their hearts,

softly layed

each Christmas morning

until eternity,

a white carnation.